CREATING AN

herbal
Bodycare Business

SANDY MAINE

Founder of SunFeather Natural Soap Company

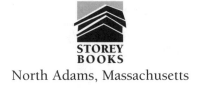

STOREY
BOOKS

North Adams, Massachusetts

The mission of Storey Publishing is to serve our customers
by publishing practical information that encourages personal independence
in harmony with the environment.

Edited by Deborah Balmuth and Nancy Ringer
Cover design by Eva Weymouth and Meredith Maker
Cover photograph © Nancie Battaglia, taken in the garden of
Annoel Krider, Lake Placid, New York
Author photograph on back cover by Jerry Frishman
Inside photograph by Jack Huhnerkoch
Text design by Mark Tomasi
Text production by Erin Lincourt
Line drawings by D. W. Roth
Indexed by Hagerty & Holloway

Printed in the United States by Versa Press
10 9 8 7 6 5

Library of Congress Cataloging-in-Publication Data

Maine, Sandy, 1957–
    Creating an herbal bodycare business / Sandy Maine.
        p.   cm. — (Making a living naturally)
    Includes index.
    ISBN 1-58017-094-3 (pbk. : alk. paper)
    1. Toilet preparations industry—Management.   2. Dermatologic agents industry—Management.   3. Cosmetics industry—Management.   4. Pharmaceutical industry—Management.   5. Natural foods industry—Management.   6. Herb industry—Management.   7. New business enterprises—Management.   I. Title.   II. Series.
HD9970.5.T652M34   1999
668.5'068—dc21   98-30916
                                                                                                            CIP

contents

DEDICATION

*To my mother, Ruth Smithoover, who through her
exquisite grandmothering skills gave me the quiet to be
the writer she always said I should be.*

ACKNOWLEDGMENTS

*The clarity of this book may not have been possible
without the assistance of my kind and noble steed Lucy.
It was with the life-breath of fresh mountain air flaring in
our lungs and nostrils that ideas came together.
It was in the shared moments of beauty and peace,
sweat and toil, that the journey of writing a book was
made possible.*

the
collective
art
of good living

If everybody ain't happy, ain't nobody happy.

— Anonymous

What is a good life made of? Addressed to the individual, the answers to this question may seem simple: Food. Water. Shelter. Love. But I believe that in this time and place, we must stretch beyond our normal individual boundaries and begin to view our personal happiness within the realm of the collective well-being of the world.

As we all know, the electronic "World Wide Web" is upon us. Over the faceless and anonymous Internet, we are truly speaking mind-to-mind with the cohabitants of our earth, with all classifications and labels — gender, race, nationality, ethnicity, age, religion, and numerous others — simply nonexistent. Is it not possible that this powerful medium for communication will become a model for the collective realization that we are truly "connected"? Indeed, connected in more ways than one fiber-optic cable will allow!

Isn't it possible that as we sit at the edge of the new millennium, speaking electronically with our neighbors far and wide; reading the poetry and prose, seeing the art, and hearing the music of writers and artists surfacing from the far regions of the world; and hearing the voices of those who had previously worked under strict censorship, that a collective inner knowing is slowly awakening within us? An inner knowing that says that individual happiness is contingent upon and connected to collective happiness?

With this sense of the world, knowing ourselves and our circumstances, beginning to know others and their circumstances, and perhaps fearing for the times ahead, the question of what makes a good life becomes more complex. For starters, how about:

THE EARTH IS OUR LIFE-GIVING SANCTUARY

- A safe and happy world teeming with diverse, sustainable ecosystems and prosperous, peaceful human cultures
- Living within the biological and ecological constraints of our planet
- Living a low-consumption (yet rich) life based upon need, not greed
- Meaningful work that contributes to our own well-being as well as the well-being of others
- An accessible, caring community of friends and family of all ages
- Daily contact with the beauty of nature: water, plants and trees, animals, fliers, swimmers and crawlers, sun, moon, stars, the food that nourishes us, and the soft fragrant Earth herself
- Plenty of fresh air, fresh water, and meaningful exercise
- Facing challenges, learning, growing, and sharing knowledge
- Simple pleasures, a comfortable pace, peaceful slumber, and love
- Mental, physical, and spiritual health

Need I say that we live in trying times? How many of these essential ingredients are missing from your quotient of good living?

Ours is an age when many of us feel that in our quest for the conveniences of *modern living,* we have lost our daily connection to *natural living.* While it once was common for people to spend great amounts of time out-of-doors tending to the seasonal chores of survival, we now find that we have given up these "laborious" toils in exchange for work that rarely offers a fresh breath of air or a drop of sunshine. Children who once worked together with their families during hours of essential and meaningful work now find themselves sedentary, idle, and often addicted to electronic entertainment of questionable value.

It seems apparent to many that we are quickly growing out of control in a world that is no longer of our own desire. Greed, crime, poverty, environmental degradation, global warming, overpopulation, and violence preoccupy our newspapers, magazines, daily radio and television broadcasts, and, subtly, our minds. As we look about us, as we examine what we do and what we wish we could do to make a positive contribution to our world, it is becoming more and more apparent to many that our existing social institutions are incapable of addressing these serious and worrisome challenges in a timely manner.

Economics for Change

For many, the solution to these problems lies in the power of economics to effect change. A voice calling for change and supported by strong economic proof that change is necessary, good, and profitable becomes a powerful catalyst for altering the way in which the world operates. If one hundred businesses found that decreasing the amount of their pollutant emissions by 20 percent in turn increased their efficiency and increased their consumer approval ratings, would not another hundred businesses take notice and attempt the same? And if those hundred businesses also increased efficiency and consumer approval ratings, would not a thousand businesses sit up and take notice? The power for such radical change lies within us, the consumers and would-be business owners of the world.

Economics is a system of global relationship, opening doors between individuals and between nations. It is one of the major forces shaping society today. And small businesses are an important, ever-growing component of our global economy.

Around the world, thousands of people are quietly striving for a better day and a better way by rebuilding the economic face of society, by building businesses and new economic institutions that support not only healthy societies but also a healthy environment. These small-business creators and owners are working in cooperation with their social and ecological communities to lead an economically and financially rooted movement for a healthy, sustainable future for ourselves, our children, and our earth. They are taking control of their own health, wealth, and bodies as they strengthen, enhance, and heal

CHANGE IS GROWTH

themselves, their societies, and the earth emotionally, economically, spiritually, and physically.

Building Your Own Business

Some readers may think of this as a "how to" book, but I would prefer that you think of it as a "how can" book.

How *can* you imagine a positive future for the world and then feel empowered to help create it with your own labor and business ideas?

How *can* you access your deepest creative desires and then integrate them into your everyday life of work, play, and rest?

How *can* you identify and let go of your fears?

How *can* it be done?

The answers resound through the writings of those who have tried and succeeded. In this book, you will read the words of simple people very much like yourself who were willing to envision a sustainable and positive future, believe in their visions, and work hard to bring those visions to life. As they set about making their visions real, many of them describe feeling in touch with inspiration from a higher source.

As entrepreneurs, the small-business owners who contributed to this book were willing to go forward without a concrete guarantee or promise of success because they faithfully viewed life as an adventure of learning and growing. Being in business is truly an experiential adventure in holistic self-education. By starting and growing a business, you'll learn many skills, including self-discipline, organization, team playing, bookkeeping, managerial and financial planning, marketing, selling, and so much more! Businesspeople learn to trust in their faith and instincts and, at the same time, learn how to compensate for their weaknesses. By honing these very skills, they gain comfort and ease in not only the world of business but also everyday life.

My business has prompted me to seek the solace and wisdom of nature and to become an artist, a philosopher, a writer, and an architect of many dreams. It has given me a fertile ground from which to grow, learn, and explore. By building your own business you'll create the freedom that you need to live by your highest values and sensibilities. By nature of the example that you set for others, you can become a beacon for positive change at a time when widespread change is imminent and essential.

Healing Ourselves and Others

Business is a vast and powerful web of communication that links many people. Unquestionably, it is one of the richest media from which new ideas and ways of being in the world may grow. Natural bodycare businesses and practitioners, in particular, hold great promise for the world. Their products put people in touch with the healing spirit of self and nature. Their services help strengthen, balance, and enhance the functioning of clients. Energized and renewed by these conscious connections with nature, bodycare producers and recipients alike gain strength, integrity, and perspective, and move out into the world on a mission of hope and healing.

Natural care of the body is an age-old preoccupation but its recent popularity has blossomed voluminously. The impact of this simple grassroots "industry" is quiet and yet incredibly powerful!

Creative expressions of fascination with natural body care are manifesting in small, often home-based businesses that produce soaps, lotions, potions, powders, balms, and much more. Other natural bodycare practitioners are operating massage businesses, health salons, and educational forums. These small companies are supported by appreciative patrons from every walk of life. Every day, aromatherapy, spa, and massage centers are catering to the thousands of people who seek greater meaning, health, upliftment, and fulfillment in their lives. People enjoy the quality and creativity of these specialty products and services and they enjoy the good feeling of knowing that they are supporting a "small is beautiful" business.

Should you require further proof, walk into any gift boutique, specialty shop, or natural food market. There, you will be certain to find the goods and services of a wide variety of natural food and bodycare businesses. According to a 1997 market overview published by *Natural Foods Merchandiser*, the estimated sales for natural personal care products were $443.1 million. The overall sales for personal care products reached $3.5 billion. The natural food and bodycare industry accounted for $14.8 billion in sales in 1997 and is experiencing an annual growth rate of 15 percent. This is quite an amazing achievement for an industry that is barely twenty years old!

What in the world is energizing this trend and what does it all mean? Well, I think I have an answer, and what a good answer it is!

the
creative
art
of business
philosophy

creating
work and culture

Since the beginning of human culture, work has occupied our days, and often our nights, individually and collectively. As creatures of comfort, we humans have endeavored to maintain a continuous process of creating material and emotional security for ourselves, our families, and our communities. This is what we consider "meaningful work." Cultural ways of being, having, and doing have evolved out of our strong need for meaningful work.

Today, many of us are searching for meaningful work, or for ways in which we can redefine the work we already do as meaningful. Hundreds of years ago, "meaningful" had a very simple definition that revolved around acquiring the necessities of basic comfort and survival. But as culture and humanities consciousness evolves, so too does our definition of "meaningful." We no longer work simply to eat well and sleep safely; we hope for a full quotient of "the good life" (see page 3).

Thoreau once said, "Most men would feel insulted if it were proposed to employ them in throwing stones over a wall, and then in throwing them back, merely that they might earn their wages. But many are no more worthily employed now." Thoreau spoke to the difficult realities of life during the late nineteenth century, yet today his words remain an echo that resounds for thousands of people who feel they are living unfulfilled lives in this postindustrial consumer age.

As human society has moved away from a balance of meaningful work in daily interaction with the rhythms of nature, we have inadvertently stepped away from that which nurtures and completes the human soul. We don't pay much attention to the difference between night and day, winter and summer, rain and sun, the cycles of nature and the human body that were once part of what shaped our daily lives. For the past three generations, human interaction with the natural world has been interrupted and often replaced by fast-paced living in a consumer-oriented culture. Perhaps it is this very interruption that has thrown us off balance and spurred our dissatisfactions with ourselves, our lives, and our work.

The good news is that people are awakening to a strong desire for a more wholesome future, and they are beginning to realize that it is within their power to use conscious thoughts and actions to envision and create a sustainable and enjoyable planetary future, both individually and collectively. With this broadening awareness, we can safely assume that the present is ready to welcome and embrace a change in the purpose and definition of "work."

It is not difficult for even the average visionary to imagine that the most meaningful work of the future will be work that successfully provides the world with positive products, services, and social changes. What is this vision of "positive" that we wish to hold in our hearts and manifest in our lives? "Positive" is a safe and happy world teeming with diverse ecosystems and human cultures. "Positive" is living within the biological and ecological constraints of our planet. "Positive" is creating a sustainable future with hope and opportunity for all life. A positive lifestyle is one that allows the luxury of knowing that all human, animal, and plant life can survive and flourish cooperatively.

I like to think of work as a transformational tool driven by our individual and collective thinking. As we look back on the past, it is easy to see how successfully those who have gone before us envisioned, nurtured, and created consumer culture. Now, as we grow beyond our need for consumer culture and envision instead a positive global future, we can be equally inspired and exuberant about our own ability to nurture our ideals and build a new global community.

The creation of meaningful work must be based upon our deepest emotional and physical needs. The movement for meaningful work must slowly build a new culture that thoughtfully and creatively addresses the current and future needs of our ecosystems and human communities.

The transformation of work in our society has *already* begun. One need only to look at small-business start-up statistics and popular literature to see that a trend in "self-determined work" has swept the country over the past decade. Thousands of proactive businesses are being created every year to meet the growing needs of people who wish to make a difference in life for themselves and for their global community. Who are the people inspired to take these tasks upon themselves? I think I know.

Welcome the Cultural Creatives

A new cultural group has already shown its face and has been recognized by the pollsters and social scientists. These "cultural creatives," as named and defined by social scientist Paul Ray (who details his discovery in a study called *The Integral Culture Survey: A Study of the Emergence of Transformational Values in America* [Institute of Noetic Sciences, Sausalito, California, 1996]), comprise a wide and growing segment of our population with many goals and values in common. Among others, they share a commitment to ecological sustainability, alternative health care accessible for all, gender equality, the revival of family and community relationships, spiritual growth, and service to others. According to Ray, cultural creatives now constitute 24 percent of the population.

You may recognize the face of the cultural creative as you read his or her want ad in the personals: "[28- to 50]-year-old seeks allies concerned with health for self and environment, who respect the feminine perspective, seek the spiritual, enjoy a multicultural and ecumenical perspective. Join me in creatively seeking ways to reclaim (in a holistic, peaceful way) our personal power that has been unwittingly relinquished to failing political, social, religious, and medical institutions of the twentieth century. Persecutionist religious zealots and patriarchal dogmatics need not reply."

Up until now, the face of the cultural creatives has been hidden, their strength has been undefined, their power as a strong social force has remained untapped. As undetected as they have been, the cultural creatives stand to write delicious history as surely as the Renaissance followed the Dark Ages.

Sound agreeable? If so, read on!

Back to the Roots

Cultural creatives are people who *need* meaningful work or they're just not happy. In fact, happiness is so important to them that they want everyone else to be happy as well. Their thinking goes like this: Whether aware of it or not, members of human, plant, and animal communities feel each other's pain and each other's joy. Fully realizing that all life on earth and the earth itself are connected, the more happiness one can create in the world, the better the world will be for all.

Their belief in these tenets is evidenced by the fact that many have chosen a work life that helps people to have happy minds and bodies. This simple philosophy is having a great ripple effect, healing both individuals and commerce, as new bodycare micro-enterprises spring up in the homes, garages, storefronts, and small factories of the leaders of this movement. Many of these leaders are not classic examples of business owners. They have been artists, philosophers, healers, dabblers, and social transformationists. And yet, unlikely as it may seem, they are finding success in their own bodycare businesses.

Since I, an artist and social being by nature, have been able to develop just such a business without a bit of business education, I believe that business *can* be a creative art. I have even discovered and defined a "creative art of business" philosophy, which I feel will work well for anyone who uses it. It is simple and commonsensible, though perhaps incomprehensible to pragmatic "by the book" types. However, even the staunchest businesspeople admit that the most successful businesses are often founded on the creative visions, artistic inspirations, and hard work of forward-thinking people rather than accounting principles or business scientists. (Those types can help run the businesses after we creative artists have birthed them something meaningful to work with!)

Yes, business as a creative art form is fun and personal, rich in relationships, and rewarding in many ways that cannot be measured monetarily.

Budding traders take heart! Trade and commerce can be as simple and fulfilling as gardening. They have been an enjoyable human endeavor for thousands of years, and when taken back to their original self-reliant roots, trade and commerce can be accessible, enriching, meaningful, and enjoyable once again. A very large harvest of abundance and joy can come from a very small garden, and the same is true of a small business endeavor.

Tapping your inherent gifts and creative energy to use work as a means for achieving personal and community enrichment is a way to make life well worth living. These are the basics of my abundance-oriented "creative art of business" philosophy. It unveils business as a garden, a piece of social artwork, and a wishing well of abundance for you and every human culture, every species, and every bioregion upon the earth.

a call to garden: growing your business

In this book, I wish to share with you the creative and organic process of birthing and sustaining a business. It is a simple process, very much like gardening, and it is one that I believe is vital to the future economic, social, and environmental well-being of ourselves and our beautiful living planet.

A garden is a place where humans initiate, define, and direct a cocreative process with nature in hopes of working for and obtaining some form of desired abundance. The most artistic gardeners listen to the quiet directions of the spirit within nature and desire to accomplish what that spirit asks of them. By listening to the wisdom of nature, the artistic gardener is able to continuously perpetuate his or her garden in harmony and balance.

The same can and should be said for a small business.

Let us demystify business! Let us take business back to its original human inclinations and inspirations. Let us look at business and its opportunities in the simplest terms so that more people will feel comfortable approaching it and using it as the vehicle for bringing their dreams, aspirations, and beliefs to life.

Let us use our most dazzling creativity to shape businesses that wipe out greed, stamp out inequity, and replace all of the things in the world that no longer serve the highest possible good! Let us use business to heal ourselves and our beautiful planet. Let us use business to support all people in bringing forth their greatest and most noble gifts.

The Tools You'll Need

Stop waiting for tired social and economic institutions to figure out where we should go next. *They* offer no hope, but tomorrow does. Tomorrow *you* can wake up with an idea for something better. *You* can plant that seed, nurture it, and watch it take root and wing. We will all be the better for it just as soon as we begin.

The tools you need to make your business garden grow are already a part of you. You simply need to become aware of them and cultivate them to become the guiding vision and action for the abundance in your life.

Gardening Tool #1: An Awareness of the Creativity and Spirit within You

Time: September 1970, age 13
Place: First day of seventh grade, Rushville, NY

A beautiful teacher appears in homeroom. Above her head there is a nearly visible golden halo of light following her every motion. She turns to write something on the board and everyone gasps! There in plain sight protruding from the back of her flowing blue dress are two white wings! The twenty-seven teenagers in the room are at once quiet. Their feet are on the floor, they are sitting up straight, and all eyes follow the graceful sweep of her arm. Using the flat side of the chalk, her wide, fluffy letters flow together like an endless ribbon of clouds.

CREATIVITY AND SPIRIT LIVE WITHIN YOU

The room is so still, with no promise of breathing again until the *words* she is writing unfold. Some of us begin to wonder if we were somehow bused to the wrong school. But then we are drawn back into the spell of who we were to become.

There before us unfurled on the chalkboard were her words: "Good Morning, Children, Awaken to Your Dream."

My teacher, and her vision for us, was a great and wonderful transformative influence in my life. Of course, there weren't any wings, and there wasn't any halo, but as I remember her and the effect she had on all of us that first day of school, she may well have been hiding them under her dress! For me, this experience was the beginning of an awakening to the gardener in me — the part of me that reaches into the elements and dream-seeds of my soul to bring forth renewal, sustenance, abundance, and beauty.

Before you can begin to bring beauty into the world you must take stock of your soul's purpose, desire, and destiny. You must find a way to recognize your inherent gifts and then celebrate them in your life and work.

Affluenza

Modern culture in North America has not nurtured our ability to know our hearts and souls. Our culture prides itself in basic tenets of freedom of religion, speech, thought, and action; yet how free are we from the intensive psychological assaults of megalomanical consumerism and leviathan media? The capitalist system worked fairly well when the world was less populated, when land-based economic power belonged to everyday people. But as megacorporations evolved, civic life devolved. The healthy precepts of diverse communities, families, and individuals are fading away and disappearing quickly. Affluenza, as cultural creatives call the current economic trend of consumerist hedonism, threatens to make our great free society into a monoculture of people with excessive needs and predictable tastes and buying patterns programmed via mass media advertising. All of this at the cost of a healthy and viable future!

The only antidote to affluenza is to remove ourselves from the nonstop static of our consumer culture, go deep within ourselves to find and tap our inner creative spirit, and then find a medium for best expressing it. Finding our true selves, beyond all of the pressures and impetus formed by media and advertising, allows us to open up and become creation- and action-oriented, to become more than passive observers of the world around us. Knowing ourselves to be creative beings, we find the motivation to become participants and wellsprings of passion, inspiration, action, and change in our world.

Connecting with Yourself

For starters, let's turn off the VCR and the television. Let's get them out of the house. Let's explain to our family members that we are pulling the plug on the most incredible brainwashing, time-wasting machine that ever has been or will be. Let's go cold turkey!

Lets start a TAA (Television Addicts Anonymous) group. Hey, now there's a business idea! See? It's working already!

"Oh no!" you are saying, "What about the nature and wildlife shows? What about the educational children's shows? What about the nightly news? Surely you see no harm in them!"

But surely I do! If you want to connect with the wisdom of nature and the deep reservoir of creative light within you, you must remove as much of the mental static and chatter from your surroundings and your life as you possibly can. Take an inventory. What else is preventing serenity and solitude in your life? Ax it!

Tell your family and yourself that it is a three-month experiment. Spend your newly found free time and money (non-television watchers spend 15 percent less of their time and income on shopping — guess why?) on getting to know yourself and your family.

Spend time connecting with the great outdoors and the world of plants, rocks, and animals. Urban dwellers especially need to seek out the natural resources of parks, arboretums, and zoos. Allow your eyes to soak in the beauty of creation *wherever* you can find it. The Discovery Channel just can't hold a candle to the real thing. The more time you spend breathing with, looking at, and being with the real thing, the more real you will become. The more tuned-in you become to Nature, the better she will be able to speak with you and inspire you. It's just as simple as a walk in the woods. The dream of reality awaits you. Awaken to your dream!

Gardening Tool #2:
A Balance between Nature and Business

Once you've brought yourself to a new, uncluttered awareness of yourself, you may wonder how you can reconcile that new awareness with your desire to return to the consumer world and start your own business. In order to do that, you need to create a healthy relationship between natural living and your business.

SEEK A BALANCE BETWEEN NATURE AND BUSINESS

Begin by purchasing a few basic items. One would be a simple reference book on basic business skills (*Small Time Operator*, by Bernard B. Kamoroff, is a classic). You will also need some accounting ledger paper, plain paper, pens, a receipt book, and a notebook. (And if the philosophy of natural health and living is a new concept to you, you may want to wander over to the Natural Living section of the bookstore. There is a lot to learn about tapping into the power of nature for health and well-being!)

You may be feeling that I am taking you into the theater of the absurd. You may even be thinking "How can a consumer culture be healed by my action of starting a business? Isn't this just going to make everything worse?"

My answer is this: As soon as you step out of consumer culture and into a more holistic and naturally (divinely) inspired mindset, you will begin to see the many opportunities that exist for people who wish to transform consumer culture into postconsumer resources! Nature has taught us over and over again that *life wants to survive!* As soon as you open your heart and mind to the light of natural life, it will guide you and your business in a perfect and powerful way, allowing you to tap your inner resources and balance them with pragmatic business acumen.

Evolution and revolution happen from within, so to me it makes perfect sense to overcome fire with fire. It's just that our kind of fire supports a sustainable happy future! Our kind of business creativity has the potential to inspire, inform, and transform corporate entities into kinder and gentler beasts!

Imagine yourself as a grand old sugar maple tree. (Take a few hours and go take a nap under one if you can.) Feel your roots deep in the earth, soaking up the water of the heavens and the nutrients of the earth. Feel your limbs reaching up toward the sunshine, feel your body and soul turning rain and darkness into sweetness and light — your gift to the world. As a natural bodycare business owner, you will transform gifts of the earth into gifts for humanity while working in cooperation with and preserving the natural world from which the gifts come.

Gardening Tool #3: A Positive Frame of Mind

Planning, preparing ground, planting seed, cultivating, weeding, watering, and reaping the benefits from your life's work is an entirely unpredictable journey. The sooner you make peace with that truth and learn to enjoy the adventure of it, the sooner your life's work will become a great adventure. Adopt the persona of a courageous explorer with a mission in mind. You, a twenty-first-century explorer, travel into previously unknown territories, never certain of outcomes. With faith and confidence, you fully expect your journey to be exciting and personally enriching. To the degree that you are able to hold this concept in your heart and mind, you will experience unlimited enrichment and joy.

THE GOOD MIND

Your security will *not* come from an ability to control or manipulate the desired outcome, but rather it will flow from your sense of mission to others, your creativity, resourcefulness, willpower, initiative, courage, endurance, and faith. This is a frame of mind you must adopt and nurture. Talk yourself into letting go, into becoming flexible, watchful, and unflappable.

If you are a cautious person, you will need to work on taking chances. Take small ones until you learn to trust the process. Risk taking is something that your intuition and faith should guide. Its purpose is to take you into new territory and to keep life interesting. I had to make a deal with my logical mind because it was throwing water on every burning desire I had to take a chance. I promised my logical self that I would never take a risk large enough to destroy me or my work. From then on it was easy to learn the joy of taking chances!

As the saying goes, you must always look for the silver lining. There is no such thing as failure when every experience in life is viewed as a challenge and a gift of learning and enrichment.

Some cultures refer to this sort of positive attitude as "The Good Mind." The Good Mind allows action informed and tempered by a set of concepts that support goodness and ease in life. The Good Mind is imbued with a strong sense of humor and the ability to be amazed and appreciative of life's many challenges. The Good Mind will preserve and build self-esteem, inspiration, and personal and collective power. It will embrace imperfection as an ally and a strength from which to move forward in a good way. A positive, courageous, flexible, and good-humored frame of mind is essential to a happy and meaningful work life.

Gardening Tool #4:
Your Inner Wisdom

Perhaps you are reading this book because you are interested in creating meaningful work and are attracted to body care, nature, and the healing arts. Perhaps you have had very little formal education in business and you are feeling the impossibility of your desire to create a business.

THINK WITH YOUR HEART

I am here to tell you not to sweat the big picture. If your intuition is directing you toward your own business, then listen to that inner wisdom. You do not need a formal business education to begin. What you *do* need is what you already have — an inspiration and a desire from deep within.

If you are founding your business on the principles of creative art, you must learn to close your eyes, visualize the form of your desire, and ask for and receive intuitive guidance. Some may pray, some may meditate, some may follow their hearts while others follow their gut-level instincts. Whatever works for you, I can assure you that your intuition is your greatest ally.

According to Sonia Choquette, intuition means "inner teacher." In her book, *Your Heart's Desire,* Sonia explains simply that intuition is about creating a connection with your inner teacher. She writes, "Intuition is not random, nor is it a fluke. It is the natural outcome of establishing cooperation among your conscious focus, your subconscious mind, your imagination, and your commitment. It is the predictable consequence of aligning your conscious energy with your intention."

If you need something, just ask for it! Stay focused on your goals and plans and be alert to how that outpouring of energy shapes the opportunities around you. The universe will provide you with whatever you need, but you must trust your intuition to recognize the opportunities as they come. The answers and gifts you truly need will rarely be neatly packaged and delivered by a next day delivery service. So you must develop your faith in and awareness of your inner wisdom and discover how to best use it. Plan on working diligently; develop trust, faith, and common sense . . . and know that the way of your Good Mind and its positive outcomes will serve as a beacon to others.

Gardening Tool #5: Abundance and Generosity

The reason for creating meaningful work in your life is so that your happy life can create good things for others. This is where the "meaning" of meaningful work comes from — helping yourself by helping others. If you feel stingy and act accordingly, you will receive stinginess in return.

The Good Mind is one of generosity and abundance for all. Cultivate a posture of internal security, keeping yourself gentle, open, trusting, and genuinely happy for the successes of other people. Aiding in the success of others is nourishment for the Good Mind. Generosity creates further abundance and further generosity and so becomes a wellspring of goodness and happiness in the world.

Work on creating ways to increase your own happiness and the happiness of others. Happiness is life-supporting and life-sustaining and therefore actualizes increase. The more you give, the more confidence you will gain in the act of giving. As abundance begins to flow to you, your ability to give more will undoubtedly increase.

Our planetary birthright is one of affluence, abundance, and infinite potential, and each one of us should strive toward it. Meaningful work, such as creating a bodycare business, is one of the most exciting and gratifying ways of realizing this birthright in our own lives and making it possible for others to experience.

LEAD ON WITH THE LIGHT

The Garden Grows

As you nurture meaningful work in your life, you will also be nurturing a new way of thinking and living that will reach well into the future.

When you discover the unique and mysterious seed that lives within, and you begin to grow it to benefit the world, you will experience the ecstasy and exultation of your own spirit. As each one of us shifts our thinking and action toward the light of a new day, so will the new day arrive.

Like the changing of a season or the growing of a garden, the process of transformation happens slowly at first and then gains momentum. The garden of social change has been planted for many years and now it is time for an abundant harvest. As old institutions become increasingly ineffective, as Mother Nature has her way, and as evidence of social decay becomes less invisible, more and more people are shifting their values.

As values shift, people begin to search for new ways to be comfortable with themselves and their lives. The shift toward meaningful work by and for the people is an idea whose time has come.

In my view and in the view of many others, business in the next millennium will truly be a social art. It will be owned and shared by individuals and groups who will, by the inspired work of their hands and minds, create deeper meaning and balance in the world. With our hands and minds we will heal the sick, feed the poor, renew the earth, and enhance diversity. We will educate ourselves in the ways of equanimity, fairness, tolerance, compassion, and love. As we use our work and our purchasing choices to relieve the world of danger and unhappiness, our own happiness will blossom.

In the following two chapters you will read about simple, everyday people who have developed meaningful livelihoods in the field of natural bodycare. May their stories inspire you to write one of your own!

natural bodycare business owners share their stories

the story of sunfeather natural soap company

This chapter details the growth of my own business, SunFeather Natural Soap Company. Just as a gardener learns his or her craft through chance, observation, experience, reading, and association with other gardeners, I learned my business in the same natural and slow-paced manner. Building a foundation of know-how and know-how-not was just as important to my success as building a market or a pleasant place to produce my goods.

Profile

Name of Company: SunFeather Natural Soap Company
Founder: Sandy Smithoover Maine, at the age of 22
Established: 1979, Potsdam, New York
Initial Investment: $15
Annual Sales Today: $1,250,000
Number of Employees
   Beginning: 0
   Today: 18
Product or Service Offered: Handcrafted soaps and shampoo bars for men, women, children, and pets; soapmaking club and newsletter; soapmaking books, supplies, and equipment; home-party marketing plan

Mission Statement

To create an abundant company that makes the world a better place through envisioning and modeling new, more socially responsible ways of doing business. To create high-quality products that inspire hope, educate, and help to heal the separation of individuals from the natural world and each other.

A History of SunFeather Natural Soap Company

The journey of learning, growing, and evolving personally as my business evolves has allowed me to sustain an enduring love for my work. As so many philosophers have said, it is not the end result that should be lived for, but rather the everyday journey.

A Youthful Wish to Live Deliberately

In 1979, at the age of twenty-two, I experienced a divine inspiration to start my own business. By "divine inspiration" I mean to say that with prayer and meditation, I was able to fully access the creative and intuitive side of myself and envision a work life that would fulfill my soul's desire to create beauty in the world. The manifestation of that vision was to start my own business.

In my childhood, I had heard my grandmother tell many stories of making soap on her family farm, and the idea had always held a particular fascination for me. I was already interested in and involved with medicinal and fragrance herbs, and when I began to envision starting my own business, these two interests synthesized into a simple realization: I was going to become an herbal soapmaking entrepreneur.

My hands were empty, but my heart and mind were filled to the brim with ideas, confidence, and faith. The energy of my body soared and I enjoyed every waking minute devoted to making my newfound purpose become real. What was my purpose? To spend my time and energy creating an abundance of multifaceted goodness for myself and others. Earthly pleasure, security, and joy were the lofty goals of my work life. Henry David Thoreau's words sang to me — I wished to live my precious time upon this earth deliberately, so that when my life was over, I would not discover that I had not truly lived.

As Faith Would Have It

As silly as I may have seemed (and certainly friends and family did their share of poking fun at me), I set upon my youthful journey with a business idea, a $15 investment, sheer ambition, and complete faith. Although I didn't know anything about soapmaking or business and had no telephone service or electricity in my Adirondack wilderness home, I never questioned these "limitations." I was happy to go to the library with questions, to conduct my business communications entirely by mail, and to produce my product entirely by hand, including carrying water from my spring. With my fifteen dollars, I bought the raw materials necessary — oils, fats, lye, and essential oils — and considered myself off and running.

I had wanted, focused on, and asked the universe for work that would inspire me, and I found in myself a vision of a livelihood that I could believe in and love. It was easy to have complete faith in my idea and in myself and I knew that my business would have an important place in the world.

A Garden in the Wilderness

As I look back upon the humble beginnings of SunFeather Natural Soap Company, I see a great paradox in the isolation of my wilderness setting. Isolation is a weakness by all normal standards of business evaluation, yet this very quiet and spiritual setting infused me with the strength, creativity, and inspiration that allowed my business to thrive from its very beginning.

There was no one around to tell me that my dream was impossible. To my eyes, there was only the beauty of nature surrounding me that cried out to be shared, appreciated, and preserved. And so it became my mission to communicate the beauty of the earth through my products and share it with as many people as possible. It was this mission that moved my business and my own personal growth and energy forward in an organic, sustainable way.

The foundation that I endeavored to build, the fertile soil from which my business and my personal abilities grew, took shape slowly over many years. These many years were filled with trial and error, large and small successes, and constant unwavering focus upon my deliberate purpose.

Nurturing the Seed

In the very beginning, or what I call the seed stage, of SunFeather Natural Soap Company (and of myself as a businessperson), I had only

myself to rely upon. I was responsible for the focus and direction
that each day would assume.
The first year of the business, I
also had a full-time day job as
an outdoor educator so that I
could earn enough money
to live and purchase the
things I needed to nurture
my dream.

EDUCATE YOURSELF

Nearly all of my "nonwork-
ing" time was taken up with
activities related to nurturing my
new business: searching for and read-
ing books on business, visiting small businesses, perfecting my chosen
craft of soapmaking, tracking down suppliers and customers, and brainstorming ideas for products and packaging. I felt like all these activities
were powerful necessities of my soul, and I was happiest when I was able
to engage myself in them.

I began selling my soaps at craft fairs, and in time began to work
with sales representatives selling my soaps wholesale. As my tiny seed
grew, it demanded more and more of my time and nurturing attentions.
So, after a year of living a double work life, I took a great faithful leap
into the unknown future. I ended my regular employment because I had
a feeling that if I could only devote more time to my inspired livelihood,
I would be able to meagerly support myself financially while fully supporting myself spiritually.

I took a deep breath and filled myself with faith, trust, and knowing. I
deliberately stopped working in a livelihood that no longer suited me and
was then free to dig into my new "garden" with both hands and heart.

It worked!

Corners, Treadmills, and Doorways

What do you suppose happened next? I worked very diligently and
effectively, and by and by worked myself into a corner — one with a
treadmill and no stop button!

Soap bars and orders and paperwork and soapbars and orders and
paperwork and soapbars and orders and paperwork . . . oh my!

What do you do when you've backed yourself into a corner? Call upon the universe for assistance, of course! So each day, while standing in front of my soap room window cutting soap by hand with a knife, I would gaze out to the beautiful spruce and white pine trees and feel the rhythm of my work pulsing through my hands and heart. Such a gift to be alive! I distinctly remember the warm fragrant breeze of summer that would waft its way past me as I worked in complete silence. I had no telephone, no electricity — no distractions whatsoever. One day in particular, I looked off toward the sun, closed my eyes, and, while still maintaining the rhythm of my work, I asked the universe to help me in the best possible way for the highest possible good of all.

Later that afternoon a car drove into my driveway and a young woman from Manhattan got out. She was part of a farm apprentice program and was told that I might be looking for a farm helper for the summer. I had almost forgotten about putting my name on such a list months ago. Hmm . . . I paused for a moment and asked her if she might consider herbal soap a cash crop?

To make a long story short, she ended up moving in with me and my husband in exchange for room and board for nearly a year. Her experience as a theatrical set builder was invaluable, as my need to build better equipment and production capabilities became an important element in the second and third year of my business. I watched this woman, who was far more capable in many different ways than I, and I learned many valuable lessons from her that I still use to this very day, sixteen years later.

The Gardener Grows with the Garden

About two years after I had started my business, my annual sales were edging toward $150,000. With my production capabilities temporarily under control, other doors began to appear and open. Behind each door was a new challenge, a new opportunity for learning, growing, and becoming.

The attractive and colorful presentation of my soap line was born from a lack of funds for printing labels. Wanting color and design as a part of my package, I found that wrapping my soap bars in floral fabric and applying a small banded label was just the answer for beauty and economy. My products' unusual and elegant look began to attract salespeople, who would call me and ask to represent my work to store owners. One saleswoman in particular had an eye for potential and she enjoyed aiding the growth of my small cottage industry. Our friendship and sales alliance lasted for many years as she sold my products to hundreds of stores. She also counseled and educated me in the many ways of marketing. Linda Raucher, if you are out there, I thank you, and I thank you again!

Living on the road eighteen weeks out of the year to attend wholesale trade shows and retail craft fairs became a great learning adventure for me. Not only was I building my company's customer base, but so too was I building my confidence and a keen awareness of the marketplace. However, as my instincts for business were being informed and sharpened, my customer base was growing beyond my ability to serve them adequately. I once again found myself working relentlessly and tirelessly.

The Fine Art of Self-Preservation

What happens when a basically relaxed, fun-loving person ends up with a demanding high-pressure business on her hands? She quickly learns the fine art of delegation! The next several years became a graduate-level course in hiring, training, and delegating work to a work force.

Where was the work force working? In my home, of course. And what did my home look like? A small factory, much like the small cottage industries in Japan that I had visited as a child. (Little did my mother realize, as she ushered me through the interesting micro-enterprises in the Japanese countryside, that she was showing me a template for my future livelihood and whetting my soul's appetite for a happy work life!)

Delegation came naturally to me. I simply made a list of all the things I did not enjoy doing or was not good at, and I hired people who seemed as though they would enjoy those tasks. People came and went, and when I began to notice that I was not good at hiring reliable workers, I handed hiring over to someone else. This proved to be a very good decision, for that "someone else" had a knack for hiring loyal, hardworking, and reliable people. Many of the people that she hired have been with the company for nearly ten years. Their commitment has been a valuable asset and has allowed the company to grow and prosper while I have kept my focus on doing the marketing and product development tasks that I am best at.

Debt and Technology

After enjoying the first five years as a home-based business without telephones, faxes, or computers, it became apparent that a larger and more up-to-date workspace was needed.

In 1984, after a contact was made for us by an impressed customer, we lost a huge order from Bonwit Teller, a prestigious Fifth Avenue gift store in New York City, when they discovered that we had no telephone. No telephone, no credibility, no order! I was not about to allow that to happen again. So we took our profits from year five and made a down payment on a renovated farmhouse, a computer system, three telephones, and a fax machine.

We had acquired technology and debt for the first time in our five-year history. But, by then, we had also assembled ample resources to manage them.

New challenges and opportunities came along with our journey into twentieth-century technology. Given my artist-type demeanor, I myself had no interest in our new computer system other than making sure that someone else did. I continued to write my correspondence by hand for a number of years and never became involved with the computer until I began my writing career in 1995.

Competition and Creativity

What did I do when a competitor came into the picture and took over a third of my seven-year-old market within a year's time?

- **First:** Lost my innocence.
- **Second:** Moved forward and discovered that creative new products could build my company in new and essential ways.
- **Third:** Sent a sincere thank-you note to my competitor for the important role she played in my life.
- **Fourth:** Discovered new ways to evolve my business mission and incorporate that mission into my products.
- **Fifth:** Became educated in graphic design and product and catalog development.

- **Sixth:** Experienced growth of 40 to 50 percent for several years in a row.
- **Seventh:** Ten years later, I made an offer to purchase my competitor's company just before she sold it to someone else.

Though she had been a thorn in my side, I was truly sad to see my competitor leave. She had been a great source of fear that I learned to transform into challenge, and a great catalyst for accessing deeper levels of creativity in my work.

Developing Professionalism

They say that the first million dollars in annual sales for any company is the hardest to achieve. Now that I understand the enormous amount of collective and individual learning that must take place before a business can truly thrive, I must agree.

As a business grows, it must concern itself with ever greater degrees of professionalism. Early on, a hands-on owner can make decisions intuitively, but a growing business requires that managers and workers develop a professional rapport, good lines of communication, and a process for group decision making. The strength of a growing business lies in the ability of its people to work together as a team for the good of the whole company and beyond. Professionalism is a multifaceted menu of learned behaviors and approaches to the daily operation of a company. It is a form of discipline that we at SunFeather are now trying to adopt as we move into the third decade of our work.

from california to the vermont highlands

The following stories were written in response to a list of questions that I mailed to nearly one hundred natural bodycare business owners. As you'll see, the respondents answered the questions that seemed to address most directly the ways in which their businesses have evolved. Many shared with me their personal growth experiences, which I hope will encourage and inspire you.

As I read the personal stories and testimonies of these entrepreneurial pioneers, an interesting and inspirational picture began to emerge. The picture that I saw included an eclectic array of everyday men and women in various stages of their own personal and professional evolution. All of them have searched for and found a certain peace by creating work to which they have a heartfelt commit-

ment. Not only have these people discovered an important peace for themselves, but they are sharing its hope and possibility with others. This, I believe, is one reason for their success. Following are their stories, from the words of the founders themselves.

LEAD ON WITH THE LIGHT

WiseWays Herbals

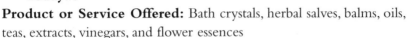

Founder: Mariam Massaro, age 44
Established: 1987, Williamsburg,
Massachusetts
Initial Investment: $1,000
Annual Sales Today: $275,000
Number of Employees
   Beginning: 0
   Today: 9
Product or Service Offered: Bath crystals, herbal salves, balms, oils, teas, extracts, vinegars, and flower essences

Mission Statement

To provide herbal products from the vitality of the Earth to help nourish and sustain the physical, emotional, and spiritual well-being of humanity.

The Seed That Started It All

My passion for the beauty of nature began during my childhood while living in southern Germany. I wandered the dense forests and meadows in search of berries, mushrooms, wildflowers, and magical woodland settings.

I read *Back to Eden,* by Jethro Kloss, and I was excited to discover herbal remedies listed for my menstrual difficulties. Red raspberry leaf was one of the herbs I used. I read another popular herbal book, *Indian Herbology of North America,* by Alma Hutchens. She listed two herbs for menstrual difficulties, and after using them for three months, my persistent problem of many years was cured. From that point onward, I've read everything I could find on herbalism. I continue to be interested in all women's health issues and have successfully used remedies for myself, friends, and customers.

History of Wise Ways Herbals

I started my first herb business, May Apple Herbs, in 1977, and also cofounded a natural-foods buying club. In 1978, I met a doctor who used alternative remedies. We embarked on a six-year partnership that began with an adventure to Asia, where we trekked in the Himalaya Mountains of Nepal, occasionally giving simple medical first aid to Tibetan refugees along the ancient trail between Nepal and Tibet.

When we returned to America, we set up a holistic healing clinic in Williamsburg, Massachusetts, that included assisting home births and dispensing herbs out of the small herbal apothecary in our home. Some of my original formulas for WiseWays Herbals came from this time when I made salves, teas, and bath crystals in small batches. In 1984, I cofounded Blazing Star Herbal School with Gail Ulrich. We taught classes in herbal medicine, gardening, and wildcrafting and sold a few herbal products under the name of Isis Herbs to our students and at fairs.

For the next four years, the challenge of supporting myself financially continued to arise despite the various avenues of work I had, which included midwifery, herbal education, and waitressing. Tired of being poor, I knew I needed to create the right livelihood to help me achieve a state of abundance. I started to focus my intention within, through meditation and listening to my intuition, to fire up the passion to find the way.

On December 12, 1987, I had a dream about creating DETOX, the first product for WiseWays Herbals, which is still our best-seller. Inspired to launch my new business, I took a $1,000 advance on my credit card and created thirteen products in time to present them at a conference on "What Is the New Age?" A buyer from a local health store expressed great interest in the products and encouraged me to introduce them to the owner. When I presented my line to him, I remember his question, "What makes your products any different than all the ones I already carry?" This question is still being asked ten years later by prospective buyers.

At first, presenting myself in the health food marketplace was intimidating, due to my lack of formal business and marketing training. My inexpensive homegrown packaging, standing on the shelves next to the professional competition, was of concern to me. However, I believed in myself and in my unique formulas, and I felt that with my driving spirit and creative abilities I could sustain myself long enough to create a successful business.

I knew from my midwifery experience that I had the courage, strength, and willingness to work long, hard hours to support my business, a very important attribute of a successful business. I like to work independently and believed that the only way to earn enough money to buy a farm, my lifelong goal, was to create a successful business dedicated to serving humanity by providing natural products for well-being. Using only wildcrafted or organic herbs, the formulas would help to restore the connection between nature, body, and soul.

My dream was to manifest a beautiful farm with fertile soil, flowing water, and a comfortable farmhouse amid peaceful surroundings — a home where I could plant my roots deep into the Earth, raise fragrant roses, flowers, and herbs, and watch the trees that I planted grow tall and bear fruit. This dream gave me the driving motivation during the challenges of the early business years when I had to hold so many loose ends together.

Although my products were being sold in local stores, I still had to find a job to support myself. Once again I turned within to ask for guidance for the next step in finding my way to a place of abundance. The next day a friend called to tell me of a job opening in the nutrition department of Bread & Circus, a large health food store nearby. I was hired as the assistant manager and herb and book buyer for the next two years. This was an excellent training period to learn the perspective of retailers and buyers — what the customer wanted, what other companies were doing — and to review the great books on alternative health care.

I continued to develop my product line, working to fill orders late at night after my young son was asleep. On the advice of the Bread & Circus new products buyer, I improved my packaging and sought out a distributor to sell my products. The connections I made there have been of tremendous value throughout the growth of my company. Several of these early contacts encouraged me to persevere, to believe that people would love the products and, in turn, support me.

Due to the rapid expansion of WiseWays Herbals, we had to move every year for five years. I worked part-time to sustain my business until 1991, reinvesting profits in the company until the business could finally support itself. In August 1993, thanks to the wonderful support of our loyal customers, WiseWays Herbals bought Singing Brook Farm, nestled in a tiny valley in the Berkshire hills of Western Massachusetts.

The business has flourished in the spacious new facility, finally separate from my living space. The quaint 1850 farmhouse includes a separate production area where all the organic herbs are processed and the products are hand-created in small batches and shipped all over the country. The warm southern slope, rich soil, and the constantly singing brook add to the peaceful charm of this harmonious healing place. Lofty maples, locusts, pines, and stone walls encircle the land. Deer, foxes, and owls frequent the meadows and nearby woods. The earth is soft, moist, and fertile here. Flowers grow abundant in the beautiful perennial and herb gardens and in the fields. Water gardens bloom with exquisite and colorful water lilies where stones, water, plants, and fish coexist in harmonious symphony with nature. Roses, the vintage roses from yesterday, display their vivid colors and emanate their intoxicating fragrances throughout the lush summer gardens.

I am honored and nourished that my dream was finally realized after all my hard work and sacrifice. I am constantly renewed and inspired by the natural beauty that surrounds me here. Living and working in such a serene, fertile, and peaceful place truly blesses me.

Each year we've improved packaging, added new products, increased our sales through new retail and wholesale outlets, and expanded the gardening areas. In order to handle our increased sales volume, in 1994 we built a two-story addition for new shipping and office areas. In 1996, Singing Brook Farm was certified organic by NOFA/Mass (the Massachusetts branch of the Northeast Organic Farmers Association).

I honestly did not imagine in 1988, when I first started with thirteen products and myself as the only employee, that WiseWays Herbals would grow to offer more than one hundred different products with nine employees and more than $250,000 annually in sales.

Important Lessons

- Maintain your uniqueness, your identity, and your spirit despite the pressure to conform.
- Carry on with perseverance, courage, and strength.
- Pay attention to the wants and needs of the customer and trends in the marketplace; stay in touch with similar businesses and read all you can to stay informed.
- You can learn whatever you need to in order to manage the next phase of your business needs, or you can find the people who will assist you.
- Believe in the presence of God, Goddess, or All-That-There-Is, even in the business world. It is an energy that flows, drives, nurtures, and supports us as we grow, step by step.

A Personal Perspective from Miriam Massaro

How do you access your deepest creative inspirations and problem-solving abilities?

Through meditation, walking in nature, gardening, raising flowers and herbs, living in the country, and taking good care of my body with natural foods, pure water, and plenty of exercise.

The beauty and serenity of the natural world always beckon me to walk amid her magic. In the stillness, deep in the woods, with freshly fallen snow upon the trees and streams, I feel the power of my connection to the spirit that guides me along in life. Through quiet introspection at these beautiful places, sometimes I hear the spirits of the plants or the whispers of the wind whistling in the leaves. I even solve my problems just by sitting on the forest floor, hugging ancient trees, or walking along the sandy, rocky shores of the magnificent ocean, where the beauty and intense power of nature inspire me to keep moving and changing, never becoming stagnant or feeling like I can't go on.

What are your definitions of failure and success?
Success is a state of mind, isn't it? Since we all have different goals for ourselves, I believe that we are all meant to achieve the abundance that we are seeking and deserve. However, success is not only financial security, but also reaches into who we are as humans. In our quest for surviving in the material world, many have forgotten the spiritual and renewing aspects of life. Some people feel they are just too busy to pray or take vacations or spend time with their families. Success, then, is a positive state of health, wellness, happiness, and a belief in your power to change your life, to develop and heal yourself spiritually, emotionally, and physically while having a positive impact on humanity.

Failure, then, would be a state of mind as well. It is difficult to help those who do not believe in their power to become successful. The first step is to remind them of their beauty as spirits, that the material gauge of success is not the most important. We must love ourselves and find our passion, what brings us the greatest joy or excitement, and follow our hearts to manifest the right livelihood for us.

THE GOOD MIND

How does risk taking fit into the picture of your life and business?
Starting a business, whether large or small, is always a risk. At the very beginning of WiseWays Herbals, I knew that the risk was not that great since I wasn't investing a lot of money, only my hard work and time.

The business, as it grows, has continued to present new risks: product liability, responsibility and accountability for all creations made under my name, satisfying employees' needs for higher pay and benefits, handling growth and financial demands, making all the decisions along the way with no prior experience, and continuing to receive inspiration and to enjoy working at what I created. Most important, the products must continue to sell and help people.

I will always believe that I can figure it out as I go, that trusting in my intuition will help and that all will work out for the highest good.

What is your perspective on formal business education?
I do not have any formal business training, although along the way I have consulted business advisers at various crucial times. I do not believe you need to have formal business training to run a business, but it does certainly give you an advantage in learning how to deal with the financial challenges you will meet.

What is your perspective on generosity and sharing the wealth of your business?
I continue to reinvest in my business, both employees and products, to improve all that we are doing, creating, and working with. I pay fair wages, provide a pleasant work environment, and, above all, create healthful, unique, and fragrant products. Developing the farm to grow more herbs and flowers organically to use in our products is another important way I share the abundance of the business. I try to support environmental causes through donations. I never test on animals. I would like to develop a teaching program here to educate those interested in the use of herbs and especially how to grow magnificent flower and herb gardens that nurture, inspire, and heal.

What current cultural practices and perspectives present the greatest obstacles to your work?
The biggest obstacles are society's overwhelming belief that modern medicine is the only way to heal illness and the government's need to regulate and restrict those who follow the alternative way of traditional herbal healing. Business owners like me always have to be careful with how the labels and promotional materials are worded and not to make any

unproven health claims. The strict guidelines being presented by the government to regulate the organic farming in this country and the possibility of Good Manufacturing Practices (GMPs) — stringent, federally regulated standards of cleanliness, weights and measures, and FDA approvals — being forced on all relevant businesses may completely change organic farming and small businesses in dramatic and as yet unseen ways.

In what ways has your business informed, formed, and shifted the world toward a new cultural perspective?
The products themselves have actually helped people to believe in the natural herbal approach in healing because of their beneficial effects. Each time I read or hear a positive testimonial on one of WiseWays Herbals' products, I remember that this is why I do this — I am really helping people to feel better without medical intervention or unnatural products with chemicals and dyes.

Today there is a rebirth in the belief in herbal medicine. In this age of dissatisfaction with traditional medical care and environmental pollution, it is exciting to witness the renewed interest in alternative health care and organic gardening methods. Learning how to use natural and indigenous herbs as remedies for such problems as colds, arthritis, and menstrual cramps is very empowering for people of all ages. This simple act alone reconnects us to nature, creating a new reverence for this living, bountiful earth that is so in need of our love and attention. We are saying that what is necessary for our health and well-being is available to us in its pure and natural state.

THE EARTH IS OUR LIFE-GIVING SANCTUARY

Herbal Retreat Center and Native Plant Preserve

Sage Mountain Herbal Retreat Center and Botanical Sanctuary

Founder: Rosemary Gladstar, age 49
Established: 1987, East Barre, Vermont
Initial Investment: I've slowly built the teaching center around me over the years, paying for expansion as it's been possible to do so. I've not ever borrowed money to see my dreams through.
Annual Sales Today: $60,000
Number of Employees
  Beginning: 0
  Today: 4
Product or Service Offered: Herbal home study education, herbal health retreats and tours, herbal apprentice program, United Plant Savers conference, Women's Herbal Conference, herbal tinctures, salves, skin cream

Mission Statement

Sage Mountain Herbal Retreat Center and Botanical Sanctuary is dedicated to keeping the earth-centered tradition of herbalism alive and flourishing. We provide educational opportunities for people of all ages that foster awareness not only of the healing properties of the plants but of their intrinsic value in the great web of life. At the foundation of our teachings is an inherent respect for the plants and an acknowledgment of their sacred plant medicine. We support ethical herbalism with less impact on our wild resources and more emphasis on sustainable supplies of organically cultivated herbs.

The Seed That Started It All

The seed of my "success" in the business realm is really the same seed that allows me to live and breathe and be a part of this great earth. That this seed sprouted into a business was really more of an organic process, a natural unfolding, than a well-thought-out business plan. It sprouted from my desire to share my love of plants and their healing energies with others. I had discovered my passion and I wanted to share that. My dream was to open a small home dispensary where herbs would be available to people in my community and where I could share with people to help them in the healing process. Since we lived way up a winding, steep mountain road it made sense to open this shop in a more accessible place. At the time there was a natural food store in town. They allowed us to turn an unused section of the shop into a small herb store.

That was in 1972; Rosemary's Garden was birthed and it is still going strong in my hometown of Sebastopol, California. It is now owned and managed by different people (who, by the way, still hold the same vision).

History of Sage Mountain

Rosemary's Garden had a small workshop space in the loft. My partners began offering small classes in the community. They became very popular and soon we had to rent larger spaces. It was at this time that I also started Traditional Medicinals, a successful herb tea company, with two other partners. I had developed a series of effective medicinal tea blends for my community, and other people began asking for them. We hand packaged them, printed the labels ourselves, and sold them to other health food stores. They took off, because at that time there weren't other good teas available. I have not been involved with Traditional Medicinals since those early days, though my business partner at the time, Drake Sadler, continued to run the tea company.

Around the same time, I also started another little business called Country Comfort. I made lip balms (some of the first natural lip balms on the market), creams, salves, baby products, and more. This company still makes quality products, but I have not been involved for years.

In 1974, a friend and I sponsored one of the first herbal gatherings held in this country. We invited four herbalists to speak, made signs by hand, and charged $25 for a weekend of classes, lodging, and meals. This monumental event was held at Rainbow End Ranch in Sebastopol, California. Fifty people showed up — we were elated!

And that was the birth of the large herbal conferences. We held them seasonally four times a year for several years. They grew from fifty to five hundred people and we soon had to rent larger spaces.

In 1982, I opened the California School of Herbal Studies in Emerald Valley (Forestville, California). People wanted more information. In fact, they were hungry for it. So you see, each step that I took was in response to what people needed and were asking for. I, too, shared the same hunger and desire for greater understanding. Since nothing like this was happening, it seemed only natural to make it happen — to create it — so we could all benefit.

During this time period I also started a mail-order business from Rosemary's Garden because so many of my correspondence course students around the country did not have sources available for getting herbs, or herbal products, or the items for making products. The catalog became quite successful. I sold it to two of my apprentice students when I left California in 1986. They eventually split the company into two mail-order catalogs, Wild Weeds and Mountain Rose, both thriving, successful businesses to this day.

On an herb school trip through the Northwest, we discovered Brietenbrush Hot Springs. One look at this beautiful, rustic, hot-spring resort and I knew we had to invite all of our herbal buddies here. The following year, in 1983, we hosted the first annual Brietenbush Hot Springs Herbal Retreat, which has become a true mecca for herbalists and has happened every year since.

In 1986 I moved to Vermont and opened Sage Mountain Herbal Retreat Center and Botanical Sanctuary. Located on five hundred wilderness acres in central Vermont, it's a gorgeous retreat center for animals, plants, and people. Here I teach classes, host events, and serve as caretaker for this wild land.

In 1990, I hosted the first International Herb Symposium, bringing together herbalists worldwide to network and to focus on traditional and modern uses of herbal medicine with an emphasis on earth-centered herbalism. I was concerned that modern medical herbalism was replacing the traditional earth-centered practices. These symposiums, which occur every two years, help to validate the traditional as well as modern techniques of herbal medicine.

In the early '90s, I became acutely aware that plants were becoming less available in their native habitats. I became increasingly concerned and walked long upon the earth, listening. Soon I knew (through a message I heard directly from the heart of the earth) that something needed to be done about the situation. I began the groundwork for United Plant Savers, a nonprofit organization dedicated to the preservation of native American medicinal plants.

In 1994, United Plant Savers was "officially" founded. We hosted the fourth International Herb Symposium as a benefit for it and were able to raise the money needed to start it.

Important Lessons

- Trust and follow your dreams above all things.
- Never worry about where the money is coming from.
- Be clear with your intent for creating something. My intent is not necessarily to make money, but to share information and follow my heart. When I get confused or feel stressed about lack of finances, I remember the intent, and I trust the process.

TRUST YOUR VISIONS

- Allow things to pass on when it's time, when there are others who can do the job better. When it's time for the business or organization to take a new step, allow it to do so, even if it means you may not go there with it. It's OK. It is its own process and you are just a stepping-stone *for it,* not the other way around.
- Enjoy yourself as life unfolds. If you are not having fun, or at least enjoying the process, then it is a sure sign that you have lost focus. Again, remember the intent, the vision, the dream, and dance along with it.

A Personal Perspective from Rosemary Gladstar

How do you access your deepest creative inspirations and problem-solving abilities?

Quiet time. I just need quiet time. To travel deep. To try to see between the worlds. To be able to listen to the voices that speak. My ability to function in this world is directly linked to my connection with the natural world. Without wilderness around me, or at least a sense of the natural world, I am unable to function well. Too much busyness is confounding to my creative abilities. But a nice long walk, a day by the sea, working in the garden — better yet, sitting in the garden — I get directly linked up and the energy just flows through me. It's divine!

What are your definitions of failure and success?
I think failure and success are simply attitudes, a personal view we each create for ourselves. I consider myself successful at something if it takes me one step closer to understanding. If one views this all as a learning experience, then failure and success are just chapters or steps in the learning process. I know I'm in balance during those times I've performed poorly if I feel a similar response when I do well. Believe me, it doesn't always happen that way, but I strive toward it. A long time ago, I read somewhere that we should seek to be like hollow reeds from which the sound of God/Nature pours forth.

How does risk taking fit into the picture of your life and business?
I think life is risk taking. To be alive is a risk. So how can one expect to be successful in life without risks? At each step you come to you need to grow and stretch. Whether it's your business that needs to grow and stretch or yourself, you usually reach a place of fright. And you'll have to risk to step through. To be creative in a business world means risking, stepping beyond what seems possible.

I use the following words, which I read long ago, as my guiding light when I get scared about how far to jump. I find that inspiring, and it usually assists me as I leap into the unknown or come to my edges of light.

> *When you come to the end of all the light that you know, and step into the darkness of the unknown, you have to believe that one of two things will happen: You will find solid ground to stand on, or you will be taught to fly.*
>
> — Anonymous

What is your perspective on formal business education?
Though I have none, I would definitely encourage people going into business to gain basic business knowledge.

A lot of "green-earth" people called into earth-related businesses are not of a business mind. As I've demonstrated, you can be successful without these gifts, but don't make it any harder on yourself than it already may be. Take some basic business courses, read some inspiring books about creative green businesses, and have good business advice available when needed.

What current cultural practices and perspectives present the greatest obstacles to your work?
As an herbalist, my greatest challenge right now is the threat to the very plants we love and use. It is a complex problem that involves habitat destruction, overpopulation, nonsustainable farming practices, logging, timber rights, and so on. We are addressing it now. It's exciting, timely, and pressing work. But I am hopeful that we can make a difference.

In what ways has your business informed, formed, and shifted the world toward a new cultural perspective?
The symposiums and conferences have educated people as to the value of the rich tradition of herbalism. I believe they have helped spread the message over the years and have helped create the current "renaissance." United Plant Savers has been a strong voice both in the natural food/herbal industry and in informing the general public of the current crisis with native medicinal plants. All of the small and large herbal product lines (teas, tinctures, herbal capsules, body products) have provided fine ethically grown or wildcrafted products. Several of my businesses have been used as models by other small businesses. By establishing my land as a botanical sanctuary and talking to others about how to do so, it is helping to create land as sacred space again. My vision is that we may all live on botanical sanctuaries before long; that all around the world in cities and towns and rural areas you'll see a sign that says "Protected — This is a botanical sanctuary!"

Starting Small

I've begun everything I've ever done by planting a small seed, watering it well, and watching it grow. I've never borrowed money for any of my projects; instead I have used that methodology whereby you take what you have (be it a dime or a nickel or a dollar) and you use that to create another. If you plant one seed, you collect more in the fall, replant them, and the following year you'll have a crop. It's not that I don't think it's good to start big, to have a lot of money to begin projects, or to get investors to back you. That's a great way too. But I like starting small and dreaming big, letting the dream sprout the seed.

Rosemary's Advice

Don't reinvent the wheel. Don't go out and re-create what's already out there. There is room for great creativity, but use your spark or dream to envision what's new, and what's needed in the world.

As I travel around to the health food stores, I am floored by the choices. I wonder how many choices we need? I would suggest, if you're thinking of creating products, to go to the large stores and make sure that what you're thinking of making is not already crowding the shelves. Now, if you think you can really make it better, better for the earth as well as better for the people who use it, then perhaps there's a need. Otherwise, take your creative spark, the genius that drives you, and create something truly needed by the world.

Consult a business adviser, and remember to talk to your spirit guides and/or the Creator about your ideas and dreams. Ask if they fit into the great plan of the universe. Ultimately any business that you start is an extension of your beliefs. So why not go to the highest authority that you believe in and be sure that is part of the plan?

Get clear right from the get-go what your *intent* is, your reason(s) for wanting to start this business. Ask the nature spirits how this fits into their divine plan. All in all, things work so much better when the universal forces are working with us. They take great delight in helping us, if they see that what we're doing is for the good of all our relationships.

THE GREATEST GIFT WE GIVE IS LIFE

Beaver Creek Company

Founders: Bruce Gillette, age 44, and Linda Gillette, age 50
Established: 1995, Fort Berthold Reservation, North Dakota
Initial Investment: $100
Annual Sales Today: $20,000
Number of Employees
  Beginning: 0
  Today: 0
Product or Service Offered: Genuine handmade buffalo soap, custom leather tanning

Mission Statement

To preserve the essence that the buffalo once represented to the native people of this land.

The Seed That Started It All

Our present business began with a dream. I had a dream of providing some of our young people on the reservation a safe place, such as a youth home, as an alternative to living in an alcohol- or drug-infested environment. Along with helping with school studies, I wanted to provide a traditional activity. What I had in mind for that was the tanning of animal hides.

After thinking and praying about this idea, I shared it with some people I knew at one of the universities for a possible grant project. My dream quickly became a nightmare. During our first meeting with the university people, I heard all the things that I could *not* do, and all the negative effects they would have on the young participants, and so on. After running into that brick wall and suffering severe blunt-force trauma, I had to lay low and recover from my wounds. But as with many of my dreams, the idea did not go away.

A year or two later my wife's father left her some money. At that time we had the option to invest the money and make 5 to 6 percent or we could invest the money in ourselves. We opted for investing in ourselves, and Beaver Creek Tanning was started.

History of Beaver Creek Company

Beaver Creek Tanning was born in August 1995. The building was erected on land that my aunt gave me for a wedding present. We bought a tanning recipe from Intermountain Tanning Company, currently located in Buffalo, Wyoming. The owner, Bernie Bickles, came to the reservation to train me for my future adventure as a tanner of buffalo hides.

In the spring of 1996 Linda, my wife, ordered a book on how to make soap. Linda was very excited about making soap for our friends and relatives. She was at our tanning shop reading to me the ingredients needed for soapmaking while I worked on a large buffalo hide. When she was finished reading this section, I asked "What's tallow?" She found the definition and reported that it is rendered fat. I asked, "How do you render fat?" She looked in the book some more and said that it is melted-down fat.

I said, "OK, what about buffalo soap?" She said "I suppose, but where do you get buffalo fat?" and I said, "I don't know, but I'll find out."

Today we are making hundreds of pounds of soap weekly from buffalo (bison) tallow and marketing it to people throughout the United States and Germany. We never need to advertise. Word of mouth, or "Moccasin Telegraph," is how we do business.

Important Lessons

- If a door slams in your face, don't take it personally! You're probably knocking on the wrong door.
- When you run into a brick wall, don't just keep running into it over and over again. Turn and try a different direction.
- A good work ethic isn't something that can be taught in school. Discipline isn't something that can be bought. If I'm not willing, able, and ready to do the work myself, there isn't anybody on this earth that will do the work for me.
- Open the door to the creator, because you can't go it alone.
- Personal health and well-being are more important than the bottom money line. I feel that my spiritual, mental, physical, and emotional states of mind need to be gauged in some way so I can stay centered. When my mind is doing all the "talking," I can't hear the Spirit.

A Personal Perspective from Bruce Gillette

How do you access your deepest creative inspirations and problem-solving abilities?

Meditation and prayer open me up to the spirit of this place, the buffalo and other helpers. It's not something that can be described, only experienced. By being on land that I am spiritually connected to (a place where my life began) I have completed one of my life's circles, and now I'm at a place where I can start another circle.

What are your definitions of failure and success?

I don't know if I have allowed failure in recent years. I have had some very hard lessons, and some expensive ones too. Failure for me would be the loss of my willingness to work and continue growing in life. When I stop learning, I'm wasting my life and that would be failure.

Success for me is every single step that I take to reach a certain plateau that I seek, there in the distance. Every order filled, every hide that I tan, every bill paid, and every new customer. Every time I feed my cat and dogs and they are full enough that they won't eat more, every time I'm able to turn on a light or use our phone is a measure of success for me. My life has not always enjoyed such luxuries.

How does risk taking fit into the picture of your life and business?

Risk taking is my life. Growing up on the Fort Berthold Reservation, I can remember times when going to the outhouse was an adventure and lesson in survival. Those of us who grew up in log houses with no running water or electricity tend to have a certain amount of "why not" in us. I look at life as an adventure, and the only way to know what is on the other side of the hill is to go to the other side, even if you are afraid.

What is your perspective on generosity and sharing the wealth of your business?

As an Arikara/Hidatsa Native, generosity and sharing is a way of life. To us, the whole purpose of life is to pass something onto the next generation. My original dream for this adventure was to pass on something to the people who may benefit.

In what ways has your business informed, formed, and shifted the world toward a new cultural perspective?
I'm a firm believer in the "butterfly effect," the idea that the wind created by a butterfly flapping its wings can affect weather patterns thousands of miles away. I may not see the effects that our products, beliefs, or influences have on the world as a whole, but I feel comfortable knowing that we are making a difference. Even if it's just being a role model to other Native Americans, youth, or businesspeople. As a business we strive to preserve the essence that the Buffalo and Mother Corn once had on the native people of this land.

Aunt Bee's Skin Care

Founder: Karl Halpert, 41
Established: 1994, Taos, New Mexico
Initial Investment: $5,000
Number of Employees
    Beginning: 2
    Today: 4
Product or Service Offered: Aunt Bee's lip balm, private-label lip balm, salves, solid perfumes

Mission Statement

To provide meaningful work and financial stability for my family and to produce a high-quality natural product at a fair price.

The Seed That Started It All

The seed had and has several facets. The primary motivation was to create financial stability for my family. I was raised in a climate of small business and a basic belief in my own ability to succeed in business. I have always been self-directed, have very rarely worked for someone else, and have always realized income-producing situations that have allowed me a great amount of personal freedom.

The idea of creating something out of nothing but an idea was, and is, very powerful to me. All of this has aligned well with my interest in natural living and ethical business practice.

History of Aunt Bee's

In 1993, my partner contacted me in Portland, Maine, with his idea for a business, which was markedly close to what we have realized. Greg had the product (lip balm), the name (Aunt Bee's), the merchandising concept (several flavors in a pop-up point-of-purchase display), the niche (honeybee products), and the color scheme.

I had several years of experience in commercial real estate brokerage and a degree of facility with business structures, due to a lifelong involvement with myriad family businesses.

I relocated my family of five to New Mexico, where I spent the first year researching the marketplace and navigating through the strange new worlds of UPC bar codes, trademark protection and FDA regulations, labeling, and raw materials sourcing.

The most difficult task of all was trying to raise seed money. We had no start-up capital; in fact, we barely had money to survive ourselves, let alone fund a manufacturing start-up. Commercial lenders would not even look at us, the Small Business Administration route was far too daunting, and we did not qualify for any local community business development or incubator funds. It seemed that we fell through every conceivable crack.

We eventually raised enough money from a few private sources to produce an initial run of a few thousand lip balms, which we premiered at the Natural Products Expo in Baltimore in the fall of 1994. We were elated to find that retailers loved our product; we were readily accepted on a small scale, with forty or fifty stores ordering displays. We were in business!

In our first year, we sold 28,000 sticks of Aunt Bee's. The next two years were spent securing retail accounts, one at a time, and gaining regional distributors as we established a presence in their marketplace.

In the course of this slow, steady, and totally uncapitalized growth, we began to get requests for private-labeling services. Relatively few manufacturers were servicing this niche. We saw the exponential growth of the natural products industry, as well as the even greater growth of private labeling, and recognized our opportunity. We knew we had an exceptional product, and began to market to firms with an existing skin care line or a market niche for which we could develop a lip balm.

At present, we manufacture for about fifteen lines, including several billion-dollar companies. Private labeling accounts for about 70 percent of our sales. We see this as our greatest opportunity for growth.

Important Lessons

- Business is highly creative on all levels. The most basic of qualities, such as faith, perseverance, and a belief in yourself, are infinitely more powerful than financial resources or "friends in high places."
- If you believe in yourself and in your endeavor with unwavering conviction, then those with whom you associate are going to believe that you are on to something, *and will want to do business with you.* Charisma, backed by integrity and a viable product, is very powerful.

- Align yourself with those that are positive, can-do types. As you begin to become empowered by your success, there will be people who will be uncomfortable with your emergence; their definition of who you are is threatened and they fear being left behind. Do not be limited by other people's expectations of who you are and are not. Be open to unexpected changes that success can bring to your life.

- Your failures and successes are your own. You are not an unwitting victim of a bad economy, lack of education, poor luck, unscrupulous people, unreasonable customers, etc. You create your own world, every minute of every day. This, for me, is the most empowering tenet of all.

- You will encounter problems, situations, and conditions completely unique to your own set of circumstances. In some cases, problems appear to be unsolvable. There may be no clear-cut answers. Oftentimes, neither your most trusted and revered advisers, your CPA, nor your attorney have answers. You, the creator and visionary, have the lonely privilege of forging your personal and often highly creative solutions to problems. This truth presents itself regularly.

- Physical and mental vitality are even more important than money in the bank. We are advocates of lots of quality time with family, regular exercise, a good diet, and spiritual balance. With physical and mental vitality, business highs are substantially more fulfilling and the lows are more tolerable.

A Personal Perspective from Karl Halpert

How do you access your deepest creative inspirations and problem-solving abilities?

Space and silence are critical to my ability to solve problems and not be consumed by difficult circumstances. My best work has always come from my least effort. The act of "trying" can often be the very block itself. I find it helpful to go to an outdoor place of natural beauty and allow time to stand still for a while. The steam room at the spa does the same thing for me.

I try not to focus too much on how a situation will mechanically work itself out. Doing so limits the infinite number of ways a situation can be resolved. Sometimes, simply allowing a process to unfold results in something great and exciting happening.

What are your definitions of failure and success?

Failure and success are completely subjective. Remaining unhappy and unfulfilled in the midst of financial reward may be failure.

Failure is usually a result of, not the cause of, depression, apathy, or loss of self.

The person who wakes in the morning feeling whole, rested, and happy, conducts his day on his own terms, finding joy and peace in the moment, and then retires feeling fulfilled — that person is successful.

In a business sense, success is having enough that those around you benefit from your success. Success is creating good, dignified jobs at fair compensation. Success is providing a feeling of safety and stability for your family and employees. Success is knowing that you have built something substantial through completely honest and ethical efforts.

What is your perspective on formal business education?

I have no formal business education. I do not dismiss the value of a business education; however, a degree alone does not give you the tools to succeed in business.

I believe that a good education in conjunction with strong entrepreneurial qualities can be formidable. An education without an entrepreneurial bent is lots of smoke with no fire.

I believe that it is important to be able to write and speak well; a command of language is invaluable in conveying the advantages of your product or service. It is also important to have an ability to deal with contracts, leases, marketing materials, and other promotional and legal paperwork.

What is your perspective on generosity and sharing the wealth of your business?

We have found it fulfilling to have created a safe and dignified workplace. We pay substantially above the Taos-area market wages and offer our crew a great deal of flexibility in their work schedules.

We believe it is incumbent upon business owners to create a work environment that they would be happy to work in themselves. As a business owner, it is very simple to reflect, "Would I want to work here?"

Following is a list of objectives for our business, the result of one of our first brainstorming sessions in 1993.

1. Produce a high-quality and effective product at a fair price.

2. Build financial stability for the organization and its members.

3. Realize a respectable profit, commensurate with the level of risk, for investors.
4. Offer financial support to civic, environmental, art, and/or social entities in need.
5. Operate in a socially responsible, environmentally sound manner.
6. Provide a safe, pleasant, and dignified workplace at fair compensation.
7. Hire and promote without racial, ethnic, gender, or social bias.

Starting Small

Starting small has been important to our survival. Starting small means that you have to be infinitely resourceful. Without deep pockets, we have had to become highly creative problem solvers. Starting small has enabled us to go for periods of time with very little cash flow without toppling.

When you start small, you become hypersensitive to the slightest fluctuations in your sales and costs — you become intimate with every facet of your business, you feel every bump in the road. We have had no opportunity to develop wasteful spending habits because there is little, if any, fat in our operation.

Starting small has also forced us to remain focused on manufacturing lip balms. We did not have the capital to diversify, which we now feel would have resulted in a dilution of our resources.

Starting small forces you to learn to prioritize ruthlessly.

Personal Growth/Family

For me, separating, or compartmentalizing my life into different sections, such as family life, work, play, and mental health, is illusory. Such divisions are nonholistic and growth-limiting. Such divisions also invite conflict among these different facets, as they compete for time and energy. I try to view my life as a whole, and balance it as such.

Balance is a key to success and survival in business, family, play, spirituality, and so on. Balance makes all such areas more productive.

SEEK A BALANCE BETWEEN NATURE AND BUSINESS

Finger Lakes Massage Group Inc.

Founders: Andrea Butje, age 34 and Cindy Black, age 34
Established: 1993, Ithaca, New York
Initial Investment: $25,000
Annual Sales Today: $1,000,000
Number of Employees
   Beginning: 6
   Today: 19
Product or Service Offered: Beginning and advanced education leading to national and New York State massage therapy licensing and aromatherapy certification; high-quality essential oils and aromatherapy products

Mission Statement

We see our educational and retail endeavors as being intrinsically reflective of each other. The Finger Lakes School of Massage and Aromatherapy Certification Program emphasizes the development of knowledge and skill, professional preparation, and working with self-understanding. The primary goal of the school is to promote personal awareness through touch and aromatherapy, inviting students to learn in a context of personal inquiry and empowerment. We encourage our students to use these programs as tools for personal growth and professional development. When holistic health care is offered in a caring, mutually respectful environment, it is a nourishing practice that can promote health, acceptance and compassion.

The Seed That Started It All

Each of us had long had dreams of working for ourselves and exploring our leadership natures in responsible, responsive ways. This, combined with lifelong interests in health, led each of us into the bodywork profession. After receiving her degree in psychology from Cornell University, Andrea moved to California for massage school in 1985. She knew immediately that she wanted to found her own school. She went on to study bodywork in several other venues and was consistently inspired by the relationships she saw among her bodywork instructors and by the impact the teachers and subject matter had on her life and on the lives of her classmates. Upon returning to New York state, she began the initial preparations for what would later become the Finger Lakes School of Massage (FLSM).

Cindy followed her own degree in health education and her career in the substance abuse field by enrolling in massage school in 1990. She felt the pull of education that encouraged a sense of individual worth and creativity and also knew that she would someday be actively involved in teaching massage, but had no idea where or when that would happen.

History of Finger Lakes Massage Group

Our dreams and passions began to truly coalesce for both of us in 1993 when we joined our energies to begin FLSM. We both continued to maintain full-time massage practices during the day, and worked late into many nights designing our curriculum and administration. Eventually we closed our private practices and devoted ourselves entirely to the school. Since December 1993, we have both been completely immersed in the creation and workings of FLSM and all that continues to spring from it.

After three years of intensive preparatory work and research, FLSM opened for the first class in the spring of 1994. The initial vision for FLSM was to offer one six-month program each year during the summer, with twenty-four students. We never had a year like that! From the moment our catalogs went out, we were inundated with requests for admission. Our first program had sixty-two students enrolled, and we soon decided to offer a winter program to meet the demands of people who were calling for information. Since then, we have run two full-time programs a year, each with sixty-eight to seventy-two students. In further response to public request, we offered our first part-time weekend program in January 1996.

All of our Massage Therapy Training Programs provide 850 course-hours of study and practice, and prepare graduates for both New York State Licensure and National Certification. As of October 1999, we will offer 1,000 course-hours, in keeping with the increase in New York state certification requirements for the year 2000.

As of April 1998, we were in the midst of our second part-time program and our ninth full-time program and have graduated more than 700 Certified Massage Therapists. As part of their education, each student has to give at least thirty free massages; this adds up to more than 21,000 free massages given in the first four years. Since massage offers the recipient at least an hour of respectful, compassionate touch, each student presents a significant offering of peace to the lives of many people. In addition to participating in a respectful clinic environment, each student also receives touch almost every day of the program. The educational process becomes a deeply therapeutic one for many individuals, encouraging their transformation into people who believe in their ability to learn, and in their ability to offer compassionate, mindful contact to others. In a culture in which touch is often either hurtful, thoughtless, or sexual, the influx into society of so many people who are able to offer mindful, healing touch feels like a great gift; we have no doubt that this work will help us become a more compassionate society.

Through our work at FLSM and our own personal study and long-standing interest in plant-based therapies, we were inspired to begin the FLSM Aromatherapy Market. Since November 1997, the market has served as both a book and a supply store for the school, as a local source of aromatherapy products and bodycare items for the public, and as a center for our exploration of essential-oil education. We have established direct relationships with distillers of organic essential oils in Europe, and plan to continue exploring similar sources elsewhere. Such unmediated relationships with essential-oil distributors and distillers assure us that only pure, high-quality essential oils are used in our products. As purity and high integrity are essential to the oils' viability as healing products, we employ gas chromatography/mass spectrometer technology in the independent testing of many of the oils we purchase.

It is important to us that all the products at the Aromatherapy Market are made only of all-natural plant material. Our world is now full of synthetic, petroleum-derived products. Many people are noticing that these substances create allergies and great health concerns for themselves and others. We believe the use of pure essential oils will increase the general health of people and the planet. We are concerned with both personal and global ecologies, and the ways in which our choices about personal health care impact the environment. It is our experience that using organic, plant-based products increases awareness about sustainable agricultural practices and promotes reverence for the life around us.

The Aromatherapy Market itself actually began in Andrea's closet at FLSM. We had begun studying aromatherapy and using the oils ourselves, which led to our desire to offer the information and oils to our friends and students. Since we had no retail space at the school, we stored all the oils in Andrea's office closet and would hold occasional sales in the lobby for students. As interest grew, students and staff came to Andrea asking for help with various ailments. The individualized blends she created commonly promoted positive change in health or well-being; the results were striking. During the summer of 1997, Andrea began to teach aromatherapy at FLSM. The response to the course was enthusiastic and inspiring, and we recognized a need for a local source of pure essential oils, aromatherapy books, and supplies.

At last, the closet was too small to hold all the merchandise and we embarked upon a more formal retail operation. We serendipitously found our current location and opened the Aromatherapy Market a month later. Our students and the public have given us a lot of positive feedback about our responsiveness to their needs. We are increasing our involvement in the aromatherapy world by opening an Aromatherapy Certification Program. This integrative program will offer 400 course-hours of in-depth education in the use and theory of essential oils, basic anatomy and physiology, and the history of aromatic plant medicine.

Our first intention is always education. The certification program and the Aromatherapy Market are both dedicated to helping consumers become educated about their health in an empowering and creative environment. Since we have both been "natural" educators for as long as we can remember, this approach is one we both enjoy and within which we feel we can authentically offer our best selves. The Aromatherapy Market has evolved out of the school itself and reflects the vision of the school, offering educational information on health care modalities which support the immune system and trust the body's own ability to heal.

Important Lessons

- Everything outside ourselves begins with an idea or an image within us. Ideas are as valuable as a final product.
- Everyone will make mistakes — big mistakes. The process of making room for mistakes, admitting them, and then problem-solving is not only necessary for the business, but also healing for us as individuals living in a society that views mistakes as character flaws.
- Having boundaries creates prosperity. No one and no business can be everything to everyone. When we figure out what we can and cannot offer, we serve ourselves and our students/customers better. They, in turn, are then in a better position to make use of our services and products.

- Most problems are problems of communication, not intention. When we take the time to communicate directly and honestly with one another, we avoid the accumulation of little misunderstandings into destructive, festering resentments.
- Taking time to rest is essential. We have the tendency to work very long hours, stopping to rest only when we notice we are thoroughly exhausted. When we slow down or take some personal time, we live more balanced lives and consequently have more energy and enthusiasm for our work.

A Personal Perspective from Andrea Butje and Cindy Black

How do you access your deepest creative inspirations and problem-solving abilities?

There is nothing like starting a huge, multilevel enterprise to force you into creativity. Before we began, we had no concept of all the details endemic to running a school, to retail, to sane and ethical management, or to being a corporation. Each of these endeavors has provided opportunities to solve problems, and each problem calls for a new solution. Some creativity feels like divine luck, landing on our shoulders just in time. We also have some very special and inspiring friends who encourage and stimulate our creativity. Taking scheduled vacations allows our dreams to resurface and grants the time to talk and organize those ideas into reality.

How does risk taking fit into the picture of your life and business?

People sometimes wonder how we do what we do. From the outside, it can look like a considerable risk. From the inside, our experience is one of following our inspirations, which doesn't always feel risky but necessary. Sometimes we look at things with our rational minds and get scared, but generally we have learned that following our inspirations leads to wonderful things.

What is your perspective on formal business education?

Neither of us feels the need for a more formal business education. Andrea has had the benefit of a father who taught business and a family that has been successful in a number of different enterprises, but we both learn best by active engagement in the projects that hold and augment our individual passions. It has been our experience that most "formal, traditional" education we have received has been stifling, uninspiring, and hurtful to our creativity. Central to our business is the desire to offer to ourselves and others education that is not only complete in content, but presented in a respectful, compassionate, and joyful atmosphere.

What is your perspective on generosity and sharing the wealth of your business?

Giving is a part of receiving. Neither of us got where we are today without the generosity of many people. As it is not always possible to give back directly to those who gave to us, we make it a point to share our money, time, and attention with others to whom we feel connected. We believe in giving bonuses, gifts, or little "extras" whenever possible. Financial offerings are one way we let our employees know we appreciate them.

In what ways has your business informed, formed, and shifted the world toward a new cultural perspective?

As a culture, we have become accustomed to taking medicines that mask the symptoms of disease or pain, assuming we are actually treating the problem. This pervasive paradigm can create an obstacle for any whole-health establishment. Natural and plant-based medicine systems, such as bodywork and aromatherapy, seek to support the body and spirit of the receiver and often take longer to provide long-term relief. This can require patience and faith that isn't always easily available to us when we are sick or hurt. In some ways, modalities based on whole-body support can ask practitioners and clients to engage in a paradigm shift, which can take conscious intention and an openness to alternatives. Because of this, it is even more gratifying to offer our community access to such proactive and empowering ways to support health and healing.

We both enjoy being creative and intuitive. We have both realized that life is much more stimulating if we follow our deepest desires rather than conform to our fears of what security may look like. It is this quality that allowed us to begin our school and store at all, and to grow them into highly respected institutions. Along with valuing our intuition, we are both very willing to undertake seemingly daunting tasks and to work long hours. We are both working more now than we ever have, while at the same time finding our lives richer and more rewarding than ever before. We are proud to be a women-owned business and to greet the world with an evolving vision and manifestation of equity, balance, and empowerment.

Employees

Having been employees for many years, both of us are dedicated to creating a respectful work environment. Our employees actually *are* the school and store, and thus deserve our greatest respect and care. We encourage our employees to be actively involved in the evolution of their job descriptions and to express themselves creatively.

The entire store was designed by the employees. We offer our instructors both the freedom to create their own course curricula and provide any support and guidance they request. We work with our employees daily and meet weekly as a full staff, making important decisions that will impact all of us as a group. We really listen to their feedback and experiences, responding when someone needs a situation to change. Trusting our employees' ideas and decisions has had a very positive impact on the business itself; we get the opportunity to witness others' creativity, employees are more satisfied in their daily work life, and customers and students feel the result of a vital and cocreative operation.

Artha Handmade Hempseed Oil Soaps

Founder: Allysyn Kiplinger, age 36
Established: 1993, Mom's garage, Concord, California
Initial Investment: $500
Annual Sales Today: $33,000
Number of Employees
   Beginning: 0
   Today: 0
Product or Service Offered: Hand, body, and shaving soap made with hempseed oil; soap made in the shape of the Venus of Willendorf

Mission Statement

The principles of Artha Handmade Soaps are to encompass a macrolevel definition of health and beauty in our product design and business plan; make items that promote health and beauty for humans as well as the rest of creation; educate about the industrial use of hemp in order to usher our society toward an environmentally based era; and use the human body and human hand as the basis for craftsmanship, rhythm, and production.

The Seed That Started It All

If I begin my search for the "seed" that sprouted into my business, I might have to look at my family background. My mother's side has an educated, professional, strong Yankee background. Plants and horticulture were a natural part of my childhood.

My father's side has a strong midwestern, working-class, self-employed, newspaperman-type character with strong-willed, independent women who always worked with their hands. I'd like to think I'm a combination of these two sides. I was raised Unitarian. I would have to say that the values of peace and social justice, in a spiritual context, are key to my hemp soap business.

THINK WITH YOUR HEART

History of Artha Handmade Soaps

I studied social anthropology at UC Berkeley. I had the opportunity to study environmental philosophy at Schumacher College in Devon, England, in 1992–93. It was there that I was introduced to the two unusual ideas that would become Artha Handmade Hemp Soaps:

- In England there were recipe books for making homemade cosmetics. There was still a vital culture of making healthy "whole food" cosmetics at home. I was fascinated with making my own beauty aids! Because of my living situation, the only thing I could not make was soap.

- At Schumacher College a young man named John from Kentucky gave a lecture about hemp, highlighting all its benefits and its misunderstood history.

After returning home to California in the autumn of 1993, I was haunted by the idea of making hemp soap. I went to the local hemp variety store, The Hemporium on lower Haight Street in San Francisco, and bought my first little bottle of hempseed oil. Almost as an after-thought, I turned around as I was leaving the store and asked if they would be interested in selling any hemp soap if the batches turned out.

On my next visit I brought in twenty or thirty weird little bars of soap. They sold like crazy. So I made more. And more and more. Coincidentally, Mari Kane was just starting her magazine, *HempWorld*. The ad rates could not be beat, and suddenly I had a nationally advertised little business.

Important Lessons

- Trust the crazy ideas, trust inspiration, and trust unusual combinations of ideas.
- Go slowly. Take things step-by-step.
- Learn to plan your finances and production schedules.
- Manage your time and personal energy as business resources.

A Personal Perspective from Allysyn Kiplinger

How does risk taking fit into the picture of your life and business?

Taking risks is a bit in my nature. I am a business starter. I love the creative process of a seemingly impossible task. I love the brainstorming, trouble-shooting, fiddling, reworking, and setting up vital systems that support order. I need big challenges. I suppose I love the unknown outcome a bit too. My real love and passion is teaching and communicating about the cultural shift that I believe we must make. Many people are saying similar things: The old ways are not working and we must find a new way. The creative forces that are pressing us and calling to us from within our hearts to invent a new way of living is a cosmological force, the force has the same source as that which birthed the stars, the galaxies, and the universe.

In what ways has your business informed, formed, and shifted the world toward a new cultural perspective?
Our society, religions, educational institutions, and businesses acknowledge intellectually that animals make a contribution, but we are just beginning to take the next jump to acknowledge that natural ecosystems also have rights and inherent value. As individuals we may know this but the collective body of society still holds individual rights as the highest law. I believe it is just a stage of evolution of human consciousness. So I trust we are slowly moving to the next level of understanding and honoring systems. I think that is where Hempsters come into the picture. Growing hemp for paper is the easiest, most rational first step in understanding the difference between using annual crops versus a principle resource such as our national forests.

I am very interested in growing my business to become a community resource, maybe as community supported agriculture (CSA) or as a co-op. Bioregionalism, and the idea of "holonic" or concentric circle economies, is very important to me. *Holonic,* in this sense, means an independent unit within a larger sphere. If you were to imagine yourself living at the center of a circle, the healthiest economy is one that relies on and cares for itself, so that as many goods and services as possible should always be purchased as locally as possible.

Very cautiously should money be spent in circles farther from one's center. If you need something from three or four circles out, then buy it, but do so only after you know it is not available more closely. This keeps local economies strong and keeps people working, which keeps culture alive and consciousness growing. For example, I use California olive oil for this reason, instead of a considerably cheaper oil from Europe or the Near East. And I'm always finding closer and closer West Coast sources of essential oils. A business should be the heart of a community and should encourage and foster the ever-budding consciousness of the people who work there. Or rather, the business should serve the people, not the other way around.

I'm very proud that my hempseed oil soap is a low-cost, super healthy, personal introduction to hemp.

Allysyn's Advice

My advice to others: start local, stay local. Build a solid base for yourself in your community. Take baby steps. Realize that your business does not have to become a mega business. The shape, size, and schedule can fit your life and values. When you do grow, don't grow too quickly. Anyone can be a flash in the pan, but it is very different to plan to be around for a few years, or maybe even a generation or two. Always stay in touch with your real, true values. And have the courage to change direction or stop if you are not enjoying it enough.

TO FIND, YOU HAVE ONLY TO CONSCIOUSLY LOOK

the
journey
begins

dreaming
and planning

Perhaps reading about the success stories of other bodycare businesses has piqued your interest and you are feeling inspired to go trekking into the world of business. If so, there are questions to be carefully considered prior to the onset of your journey. You might consider these questions a mere safety precaution, a warning, or an outright challenge. Even if your business grows to become a successful one, it will be a continuous source of difficulties, issues, and uncertainties — namely, problems! But I rarely give "problem" status to the daily challenges that business inevitably presents, simply because I enjoy meeting those challenges so much. I also delegate responsibility to others, who kindly protect me from all but the most interesting and threatening of challenges.

There are certain qualities and traits that lend themselves well to business and others that do not. It is up to you to decide whether your own vision, stamina, determination, and grit make you better suited to becoming a Fortune 500 master or a happy part-time massage therapist. Whatever your calling, it would be wise to first assess your personal panache. You can then match your business vision to the potential that you feel is yours.

The Biz Quiz

The first questions to ask yourself are hinted at in the previous two paragraphs. Can you find them? If so, you are *good at noticing subtleties,* your first Fortune 500 attribute!

The hidden questions are as follows:

Question 1

Are you likely to respond positively when faced with business "problems"? Are you capable of perceiving and responding to daily business dilemmas as challenges rather than problems?

If not, then you will probably experience a great deal of stress from being in business.

A business owner must either have or develop nerves of steel. I have a plaque on my office wall with a quote by Mark Twain. It says, "I have had a great many troubles, but most of them never happened." If not for those wise words hanging on my wall all these years, I just might have been defeated by the many ups and downs of business. His simple wisdom helps me remember to be patient, thoughtful, and proactive when challenges crop up.

Ironically, some of my worst "problems" have turned out to be blessings in disguise. Witnessing this phenomenon over and over again has strengthened my faith to the point where I now welcome all challenges and trust that they will move me to where I need to be.

Question 2

Do you trust yourself to hire people you can trust to do the things that you are not good at, or may not have time to do?

Trust is the most essential mind-set needed to be a good businessperson. It is a quality that most people will respond to in kind when they experience it emanating from you. Trusting in yourself to be and do your very best is the first step in nurturing yourself and the people you work with into being the very best you all can be. Choose people that you feel you can trust and inspire. Then train them and trust them to accomplish more than you ever could by yourself.

Question 3

Do you enjoy hard work and diligence? Will your work motivate you to work hard?

Entrepreneurs are viewed as highly motivated people, and with good reason: They usually work very hard. But they also enjoy their work. They gain a great deal of self-fulfillment and confidence from both the challenges and the results of their labor.

Question 4
Do you have good relationships with people?

Before venturing into the world of business, be sure that you are capable of sustaining positive long-term relationships with many different types of people. Good relationships are critical to good business. They are a sign of clear and consistent communication. If you repeatedly experience difficulties in your relationships with people, chances are that you will be plagued with difficulties in any business attempt.

Question 5
Are you honest, open-minded, and fair?

In order to be successful with customers, suppliers, and the hosts of others that you will encounter in business, it is essential that you hold honesty, open-mindedness, and fairness high in your heart.

Question 6
How strong is your intuition? Do you trust your intuition?

I cannot stress enough the value of good instincts. Even if you are inexperienced in business, if you are aware of your innate intuitive abilities, you're golden! You can always hire people with knowledge — sound intuition is much harder to come by. I was able to build my company for the last fifteen years mostly on faith, feel, and intuition. When it comes to decision making, good intuition can cut through hours of study, reams of reports, and much consternation.

Question 7
Are you able to communicate your wishes clearly?

There is a fine art to being direct and assertive without being abrasive, pushy, or unyielding. If people respond well when you are being assertive, then business relationships and leadership roles will be smooth sailing for you.

Question 8
Do you enjoy being a self-learner?

Self-education, such as reading, workshops, and seminars, is the best way for businesspeople to grow and respond to the changes that markets are famous for. Self-education can spur your creativity, enhance your problem-solving abilities, and keep you motivated and alive in your work.

Question 9
Do you have a family or wish to have a family in the future? Will your family want to be involved with your business?

A business takes a great deal of time and commitment. It is difficult to juggle both family responsibilities and work that demands more of you than a regular occupation. I have been able to enjoy both a business and a family, but there have been trade-offs. The support of your family is crucial to your success. Without it, you're sunk! If you do have a family, involve them in the discussion and consideration of starting a business.

Question 10
Are you a leader or a follower?

If you are uncomfortable in a leadership role and dead set against developing leadership skills, then you may want to consider working in someone else's business. Remember that even if you create a one-person business, you'll still be a leader in your customers' eyes.

To help develop your leadership savvy and confidence, I recommend reading any of the following books: *Ben & Jerry's Double-Dip, Leadership & The New Science, Stewardship,* or *The Empowered Manager* (see Suggested Reading for complete information).

Question 11
Will you persevere? Can you ride out the ups and downs that your business will inevitably present you with?

Year in and year out, you will face slow progressions, long declines, miracles, and disasters. If your will to succeed is strong and you are determined to see your business through the good times and the tough times, you'll have 95 percent of the work of getting to success done.

Question 12
Are you daring enough to take chances and willing to live with the consequences of both your failures and your successes?

Success can make life just as difficult as failure! Risk taking is a necessary game that all entrepreneurs must play. Failure is not the enemy of success. Although winning is usually fun, losing is usually instructive. In order to learn how to do things, you need to be willing to make as many mistakes as it will take to learn how not to do things.

Question 13
How will you handle the material results of your success? Will financial and personal success encourage you to become a philanthropist?

The world doesn't need any more wealthy tyrants! In writing this book, I offer whatever wisdom I have in the hopes of unleashing legions of wealthy philanthropists upon the future. Wouldn't you like to be one?

Question 14
Are you confident in making decisions? Can you be creative, innovative, and realistic in your decision making?

These qualities surely come in handy when it's time to figure something out, and when you're in business it's always time for that!

Question 15
Are you willing to ask for help when you need it?

Good professional help can pave your path with opportunities, insights, and preventive measures, which can save you years of work and thousands of dollars.

Question 16
Do you have a deep, burning desire to fulfill a certain mission in your life? Will your business help you to achieve this goal?

This is one of the top three criteria for success, right up there with intuition and a can-do, positive, "YES!" attitude. The torch of your deep desire is equally important, as it will light and energize every step of your way.

 foundations for success

The three most important attributes an aspiring entrepreneur can have or develop are:
- ✦ Good instincts and trust in your intuition
- ✦ A positive, can-do, "YES!" attitude
- ✦ A business idea that will help you to fulfill a deep-burning life's desire

If the results of this quiz have left you feeling dismal or ill-suited to ful-filling your dream of having a business, I have one final question for you . . .

Question 17
Are you capable of transforming those things about yourself that might not work in business?

If so, please read on!

Dreaming and Designing the Idea

To accomplish great things, we must not only act but also dream, not only plan but also believe.

— Anatole France

I trust that you had fun assessing your strengths and weaknesses as a potential business owner! Whether you're feeling just a glimmer of hope for yourself or you are absolutely certain you have everything it takes to be the next Anita Roddick of the bodycare world (she founded The Body Shop), the best part is yet to happen: deciding exactly what it is you want to do and how you are going to do it.

Once your business idea takes form, it will be time to plan, plan, and plan some more, which will take us through the end of this chapter. Parts 3 and 4 of this book will focus on sales, marketing, and management. But first, I would like to help you create your business idea.

There are a number of ways that a business comes into being:

- **Calling.** Many entrepreneurs feel that they were actually born to do what they do, that it is their calling in life. You may have an intuitive ability for healing with your hands, which may inspire you to become a massage therapist, or you may have always instinctually known which herbs would be good for what and feel destined to become a practitioner of herbal medicine.

- **Desire.** Other entrepreneurs decide that they want to begin a business, and as soon as that thought is put out into the universe, opportunities and ideas begin to appear.

- **Contacts and training.** Others take a more practical approach and draw from existing professional contacts or personal know-how.

- **Purchasing.** Another possibility to consider is purchasing an existing business, but I recommend that this option is best reserved for people with business experience.
- **Trend awareness.** Spotting trends is yet another way some businesses begin. Trend spotters look for subtle hints that something may eventually blossom into a popular trend. If you're really good at honing in on business possibilities, you can *create* a trend.

The best overall advice I can give you is to be aware of your own inner guidance. Sonia Choquette, author of *Your Heart's Desire,* speaks wisely of intuition: "Intuition is not random, nor is it a fluke. It is the logical next step in the creative process of manifestation, the natural outcome of establishing cooperation among your conscious focus, your subconscious mind, your imagination, and your commitment. It is the predictable consequence of aligning your conscious energy with your intention. At this stage in the process of manifestation, spiritual intuitive guidance begins to play a major part in leading you toward success."

The era in which we live is in the throes of many paradigm shifts. Changes in education, science, medicine, politics, and business speak to a renaissance of receptivity to new ideas and new ways of doing things. The time has never been riper for innovative businesses. I believe the most successful businesses of the future will address the most important and challenging issues of our time. Ecological and social repairs to the damages inflicted on the Earth and her inhabitants will be key tasks for future businesses. When the general public begins to understand that the well-being of our entire planet is the only basis for a healthy economy, I believe many consumer desires will change overnight. Many businesses will be deemed inappropriate and will die. Other businesses more in tune with the needs of our time will flourish.

So, as you dream your business idea, look into the crystal ball of the past, present, and future. Decide where it is that you want to be, where you don't want to be, and what part you wish to play in creating the economic, social, and ecological world for future generations.

CHANGE IS GROWTH

Here are some of the classic bodycare business ideas. There are, of course, hundreds more — business in the bodycare field is what you make of it!

- Acupuncturist
- Aromatherapist
- Aromatherapy or natural-products manufacturer
- Bodyworker
- Business consultant to the trade
- Catalog marketer for bodycare products
- Ceremonialist
- Clinical herbalist
- Communicator (radio, video, television)
- Conference organizer
- Educator
- Gift crafter
- Gift marketer

- Graphic designer to the trade
- Herb grower
- Homeopathic practitioner
- Lobbyist
- Massage therapist
- Oil distiller
- Publisher
- Researcher/tester
- Retreat center administrator
- Shop owner
- Soapmaker
- Spa owner
- Tour organizer
- Trade organization administrator
- Writer
- Yoga teacher

Pencils, Paper, and Crayons

It may take some time to consciously realize your business idea. Sometimes it helps to remove yourself from your normal routine and scenery. New people, places, and objects can coalesce with your intuition and synthesize into wonderfully creative possibilities. Some ideas will come and go, but one shining idea may captivate you. Your thoughts will continuously return to it and it will feel just right. You will want to learn everything you can about the idea that has attracted your attention so strongly. As soon as you are convinced that this idea is right for you, get it out of your head and onto paper. Describe it, draw it, and color it in!

What will your business do and why? Where will it be? Who will your business serve and how will you reach out to your customers? Who will take care of the business each day?

The activity of writing about, drawing pictures of, and coloring your idea on paper will actually help you access the intuitive, creative part of your brain. Try to surround yourself with peace and quiet while you work, since interruptions from the outside world will hinder the creative flow. As your hands move across the page, an outpouring of ideas and visions will come to you. Let it *all* flow out from the heart of your heart onto the paper. It will all be valuable in one way or another. Work on this project as often as you need to, until you have a solid vision of what you desire to create. Let this illustration of your ideas be free-flowing and uninhibited — a nice right-brain balance to the more traditional business plan that we will work on later.

Imagine its beginning fully and colorfully, and commit your imagery about that to paper. Think of it as a grand creation, or a seed if you like. Amazingly, this seed may grow into one of the most incredible experiences of your life. Your creation may touch the lives of thousands of people, for better or for worse. Let's plan on it being for the better!

The subtleties of your artwork will tell you a great deal. Is it methodical and careful, or wild and flamboyant? Is it messy or beautiful, playful or serious? What can your artwork tell you about how you could create a more balanced and effective business?

To consciously plan how you will and will not allow your seed to grow, you can frame your business creation with certain simple intentions. Here are three of my favorites:

1. My business will serve the highest possible good for all involved with it.
2. My business will be sustainable, giving back what it takes to avoid social and ecological harm.
3. My business will be fluid, continually influenced and enhanced by new ideas and inspirations.

Business Planning Map

A business plan is a blueprint for your start-up goals and actions. Enjoy creating your business plan. Keep it simple and believable. Let the plan create a visual image of your business, complete with graphics, pictures, words, and numbers.

If you are a novice, you may need help generating the financial reports. If this is the case, please refer to the section on working with professional advisers on page 125.

The purpose of your business plan is multifaceted. The document you create will help you determine whether your idea is worth the time and resources required to develop the business. Also, your plan may be a tool for selling your business concept to investors and potential employees. Most important, your business plan will give you an understanding of your chosen journey. It will bring organization and life to the vision you have worked so hard to create.

Prior to writing your plan, consider how important it will be to your start-up. The length of a plan may be either a few pages or a few hundred pages — volume is less important than making sure that your plan is thorough enough for your needs. Whether you are you are starting with a million-dollar loan or a shoestring budget, your plan should realistically reflect your financial situation. It will become a blueprint for your first months of operation. It should provide the details and projections for future growth. Focus on short-term operating goals in your plan, but be sure it reflects your long-term vision as well.

Questions concerning the viability of your business concept must be answered to the best of your ability. Go to the library and do some research. Conduct informal interviews. Give away free samples of your work and ask for feedback. Surf the Internet. Visit a bookstore. Call the Small Business Administration or visit a small-business development center. Attend trade shows and conventions as an observer. Visit stores, offices, and factories related to your concept.

◡ sage advice ◠

THE ELECTRONIC ENTREPRENEUR

If you have access to a computer, I recommend that you purchase a software program called Legwurks (see Business Resources on page 149). This amazing instructional guide educates the user not only on the entrepreneurial process, but also on various business topics entrepreneurs need to understand and implement. Legwurks is a perfect advanced complement to this book, and well worth the money and time you invest in it. When you complete the Legwurks program, your business plan will be done, you will have completed a crash course in business basics, and you will be well on your way to the rewarding world of entrepreneurial adventures.

In my opinion, no one but you should seek or prepare the preliminary information for your business plan. Doing this exercise is very important to your own discovery and understanding of basic business skills. You may stumble and grumble through this gauntlet, but you will learn from it. And what you will learn is essential knowledge for any creative entrepreneur.

Does your concept hold up to this sort of preliminary fact-finding and scrutiny? If so, then the next step will require some imagination, detective work, and writing materials. As you move beyond the concept phase and on to the design phase of your idea, you will need to put your best writing and planning skills to work.

Some people call this work a business plan, but I think of it more as a blueprint or a road map. This seems to be an easy metaphor for most people to grasp. Think of your business plan as your construction blueprint, complete with timetables and financial planning. Should you wish to delve even deeper, many self-help materials are available on this topic. These materials can easily walk you through the business planning process. (See Suggested Reading on page 144.)

Your business plan should encompass the following:
- — Cover page
- — Contents page
- — Introduction
- — Mission statement
- — Business overview
- — Economic analysis
- — Financial analysis
- — Marketing analysis
- — Audits and accountability
- — Summary
- — Indexes and supporting materials

Introduction

The introduction should concisely state the purpose of your business and your overall plan.

Mission Statement

The mission statement should spell out your company's philosophy and direction. It should encompass how you will run your business and how you want to be perceived by the public. Mission statements vary depending on the type of business, so be sure to emphasize the uniqueness of your product or service, your commitment to the customer, and your commitment to ethical standards and integrity. Include information about any innovative practices or technology that will make your company unique.

Business Overview

Next you will need to write a full description of the products or services you will offer and the proposed location of your business. Describe your target market (what types of people would be most likely to want your service or product?), sales force, methods of sales and distribution, advertising and promotional plans, and the possible evolution of your product line or services. You should discuss pricing, seasonality, and growth strategies.

Propose key management staff, if any. You may need to hire employees with skills you do not have. Show how you will compensate for your weaknesses by working as a team with others. If you plan to start your business with a number of employees, create an organizational chart listing each management position and defining its function.

State why your business is bound for success. Discuss what you know about your competition and what will distinguish your business from theirs. Define where you want to be in a year's time and list the short-term objectives that will get you there. Delineate milestones and set up a schedule for reaching those milestones as the business develops.

Economic Analysis

Report on the condition of the local, regional, state, and national economies in the context of your business and industry. Discuss the possibilities of seasonal fluctuations in sales. Note growth trends, legal issues, strengths, and weaknesses. Write about what's going on economically in your chosen field of business. This type of information can be found at the resource desk at any public or college library.

Financial Analysis

This part of your business plan is very technical — and very important. It will help you project income and will give you a more complete picture of your financial status and future financial goals. If you are unfamiliar with creating financial reports, seek the aid of a certified public accountant or business consultant. These professionals have computerized templates for all of the reports needed for the financial analysis section of your business plan. They can easily input information, and output professional and useful reports on your behalf. (If you have an aptitude for accounting and financial planning, the Legwurks software program can successfully guide you through this important process.) Whether you are working with a professional or doing it yourself, you will need the following information and estimates for a financial report:

- **Financial requirements.** These are the necessary start-up costs minus the amount of money that you currently have available.
- **Estimated sales figures.** Be conservative. Support your figures with as much evidence as possible.
- **Cash flow report.** List your estimated biweekly expenditures and income.
- **One-year budget.** This represents your first financial year. It should include your fixed costs, overhead, salaries, taxes, advertising costs, and leases as well as projected variable costs.
- **Balance sheet.** This will show your current net worth. It should list your assets, liabilities, and equity.
- **A "break even" analysis.** Show what level of sales will be needed to support your business, and a final statement on your accounting methods and credit policies.

 econ 101

Fixed costs are those monthly expenses that remain the same from month to month, including rent, insurance, equipment rentals, and salaries. *Variable costs* are those expenses that can change from month to month, although you will certainly want to try to account for them in your budget. Some variable costs include materials, hourly labor, shipping, advertising, and selling expenses.

Market Analysis

This section highlights the market for your product, your competition, and your methods of pricing, advertising, and selling. Discuss trends and how your product will differ in price, quality, or service from those of your competitors. Develop a thorough section on marketing strategies, advertising plans, and distribution channels. (For information on these topics, see chapter 7.)

Audits and Accountability

Describe how you will assess your company's performance. How will you evaluate where the company stands in relation to its mission and goals? Many socially responsible companies conduct "green audits" — a self-assessment tool that measures a business's environmental commitment and performance. Other audits can measure how well the company meets the needs of its employees, customers, and community.

Summary

Write a few concluding statements that will bring the entire report into focus in an inspiring manner.

Indexes and Supporting Materials

Include any flow charts, indexes, or supporting materials that will enhance the reader's understanding of your business concept. Examples of supporting materials might include credit reports, key contracts, leases, letters of intent from prospective customers, résumés, job descriptions, and recommendations.

Congratulations! Your business plan is complete. It may have taken a week, month, or a year to compile but don't you think it was worth the effort? Look at how much you have learned!

Reckoning

As soon as you conceptualize your business, stop and take a careful, critical look at your concept. Consider, evaluate, and reckon with it! Does it have the trappings of a viable and vibrant opportunity, or is it likely to become less than what you hoped for, after investing thousands of dollars and hours into it? Realistically speaking, some ideas make better hobbies or volunteer activities than businesses. If you've stumbled upon such an idea, lay it to rest before it robs you of time, money, and joy. After completing the planning and writing of your business map (either from my format or another), I recommend that you have your work reviewed by a professional business consultant, whose suggestions and insights will likely be valuable.

While you are doing the preliminary research for your business, you may also want to consider any federal regulations that govern your field. The best overview of these considerations that I've seen are in Susan Miller Cavitch's book, *The Soapmaker's Companion* (Storey Books, 1997). Her description is addressed to soapmakers, but can also be applied to many other product-oriented businesses:

"The FDA statute defines cosmetics as 'articles intended to be rubbed ... or otherwise applied to the human body ... for cleaning ... except that such term shall not include soap.' However, soap that claims to have certain cosmetic properties is not exempt.

"If FDA rules appertaining to cosmetics apply to your soapmaking, you will need to concern yourself with several rules, the most important ones being the following:

"**Labeling.** Whether or not your soap is considered a cosmetic under FDA rules, the label must indicate several things. First is the net weight of the contents in ounces. The net weight may also be expressed using metric units (i.e. grams), but even in this case, ounces must be disclosed. The label must also state the name and address of the manufacturer, including the street address, city, state, and zip code. If it is listed in a current telephone directory, though, the street address may be omitted.

"In addition, under FDA regulations if your soap is classified as a cosmetic, the ingredients must be listed in the order of their predominance. (Color additives and ingredients present at under 1 percent may be listed without regard for predominance. Some ingredients are exempt from disclosure regulations and may be referred to simply as 'and other ingredients.') The actual percentages of each ingredients do not have to be included. Also, the ingredients must be identified by the names established or adopted by regulation. The declaration of ingredients must be conspicuously placed on the label so that it is likely to be ready by a purchaser; the letters must be at least $\frac{1}{16}$ inch (1.5 mm) in height $\frac{1}{32}$ inch (0.78 mm) if the total package surface available to bear labeling is less than 12 square inches (77.4 square cm).

"Some soapmakers are under the erroneous impression that a chemical is not an ingredient if it reacted with other chemicals and is thus no longer present in the final product. These soapmakers, for example, do not think that sodium hydroxide need be listed, since there is no sodium hydroxide left in their final bars. They are wrong. *Ingredient* is not defined as a component of the final bar, but as a component used in the manufacturing process. The FDA regulations define the term as 'any single chemical entity or mixture used as a component in the manufacture of a cosmetic product.' And *manufacture* means 'the making of any cosmetic product by chemical, physical, biological, or other procedure.' Combining these two definitions clarifies that an ingredient is any single chemical entity or mixture used as a component in the making of any cosmetic product —including sodium hydroxide. The definition clearly anticipates that the manufacturing process may be a chemical one in which an ingredient reacts and is no longer present in the final product.

"If the safety of your materials has not be substantiated — for example, if you use a color additive that has not been expressly approved by the FDA — your label may have to include a conspicuous warning: 'Warning — the safety of this product has not been determined.'

"Color Additives. If federal law classifies your soap as a cosmetic, then your color additives must be tested for safety and approved by the FDA. If you use a color additive that has not been approved, your soap will be considered adulterated and in violation of the law. (Many natural colorants, such as alkanet root, rose hips, and brazilwood, have not been expressly approved by the FDA.)

"Sanitary Production Process. If federal law classifies your soap as a cosmetic, then you must manufacture and store it under sanitary conditions and avoid contamination with filth. This is a standard of cleanliness that kitchen soapmakers are not likely to meet. Sanitized equipment, gloves, hairnets, confirmation of weights and measures by a second person, sampling, water testing, absence of tobacco products — these are just a few of the so-called Good Manufacturing Practice Guidelines cosmetic manufacturers are measured against.

"False Claims. If federal law classifies your soap as a cosmetic, then you must be especially careful not to make any claims about it that are exaggerated, misleading, or untrue."

Scrutinize Your Business Concept

Take a moment to honestly assess your own time availability, financial resources, expertise, risk comfort level, and financial need. Ask yourself some hard questions. Does your business idea match your level of resources and expectations? Your values and interests? Will it help you to grow personally and realize your greatest gifts? How will your business meet the requirements of its original purpose? Is there potential for this business to make a profit? How much service or product can you produce and at what cost? How much will people pay for it? How much will it cost to find and keep customers?

What do friends, associates, and strangers think about your idea or product? How do they feel about its potential? (Be forewarned: Friends and family are often either your worst critics or will not speak forthrightly for fear of hurting your feelings.)

How educated (or programmed by advertising) are your customers? Are similar businesses succeeding? What type of regulatory or certification issues exist? How strong is the market? Some markets must be created through advertising, consumer education, and experience. Other markets have already been created but not fully tapped; still others are saturated.

After research and much consideration, some people discover that their concept holds less than vibrant potential, but they still find it impossible to let the idea go. Often when an idea becomes haunting, it does hold some incredible opportunity. It may simply need to be rethought, redesigned, or synthesized into something else. Again, it is always wise to listen to your intuition and persevere with faith while the answers unfold.

Be Wise about Size!

E. F. Schumacher, author of *Small is Beautiful,* spoke of the three purposes of human work:

1. To provide necessary and useful goods and services.
2. To enable every person to utilize and perfect his or her inborn talents and gifts.
3. To work in service to and in cooperation with others.

Schumacher placed a higher value on joyful and sustainable living than on wealth. Focusing on these goals, rather than on wealth for its own sake, an entrepreneur is enabled to achieve meaning within the context of an adequate living. This insight alone may be enough to dissuade you from trying to create an enterprise that is so big and complicated that it might defeat your own happiness in the end.

Practically speaking, if you have no prior business experience or start-up funds, then you need to start *very small*. By starting small, you will afford yourself the experience of learning from the ground up. You will build your business one dollar at a time and become knowledgeable about every aspect of your operation.

This is the path that allowed me to know more about business than I ever expected to know. I began my business with $15 when I was twenty-two years old and working a full-time, low-paying job. I learned my business lessons via experience, associations with professionals, and constantly seeking ways to keep up with the demand for my very popular products.

Starting small and growing steadily also affords you a certain degree of protection from financial mishap. As long as you never take a risk larger than what you can afford to lose, you will ensure your own financial survival. These are very simple rules, but essential ones if you wish to approach business as a creative, integrated art rather than as a money-making scheme.

 writing skills

Don't be discouraged if your writing skills are poor — you are not alone! Your ideas, creativity, and drive, not your writing skills, are the keys to your success. If you can get the basic ideas down on paper, you can always have a good writer copyedit your writing. You'll be surprised, too, at how this practice will improve your writing over time. (Details on working with professional advisers is available on page 125.)

setting up shop

Welcome to your new business! You've worked hard to get this far. You've imagined an idea, embellished it on paper, and worked to evaluate it legally and professionally. Now you are ready for your first customer . . . or are you?

The business plan is a very important piece of the puzzle, but it's not the whole puzzle. Before you begin thinking about how to build a market and manage your company, there are a number of practical concerns to consider. These include organizing a work space, pricing and purchasing, customer service, and quality control. Once you have a sense of these important business skills, you'll really be ready to set sail!

Organizing Your Work Space

Regardless of what type of business you engage in, and whether you work at home or in a rented office, you will need a well-organized place to do your work. An office is the hub of your business. Ideally it should be located in a space that is close to but separate from your production or service area. A separate space will assure privacy and quiet. If you are offering a service, you'll want a reception area as well as a behind-the-scenes business office.

Though I began my business without a computer, phone, or fax machine seventeen years ago, I would not do so today. The amount of communication, information, and marketing power that these office tools offer is indispensable. If you are not computer literate, find people who are and learn from them. At the very least, your office should house:

— a phone and answering machine
— a fax machine
— a file cabinet
— bookshelves
— office supplies
— a desk
— comfortable chairs

Organizing Your Records

Choosing between a paper or electronic filing system will depend on your budget and degree of computer literacy. Computers are great repositories for stored information, but that information must be managed by a savvy computer person. If you are a one-person operation with a minimal budget and minimal computer skills, then I would recommend managing your information the old-fashioned way — with files. As your business grows, you can work toward becoming more computerized.

A simple file system includes the following drawers or computer files:

- **Accounts payable.** Divide this into three sections: pay ASAP, pay within thirty days, and pay within sixty days. Arrange each section alphabetically. Update your payables weekly. Each vendor gets its own file folder.

- **Paid invoices.** Set up an alphabetical file with a folder for each vendor. Whenever an invoice is paid, mark the date and check number, and file the paid invoice.

- **Purchase orders.** Create a purchase order form (see sample in appendix) for every item you order. Keep purchase orders filed alphabetically by order name until the purchase arrives, then attach the packing list to the purchase order. Check the shipment for accuracy; any problems or discrepancies must be addressed. Attach the purchase order and packing list to the invoice, making sure that the invoice is accurate.

- **Pending orders for goods or service.** This file should include appointments for service or orders for goods from your customers and should be arranged alphabetically by the customer's name.

- **Fulfilled orders.** All fulfilled orders should be filed alphabetically by customer's name. Each file becomes a historical record of sales activity for each customer.
- **Accounts receivable.** Each time you sell, you must create an invoice that details the sale, the customer, the delivery date, the financial terms of the sale, and any miscellaneous information. All invoices should be filed alphabetically with a flag detailing due date. All late payers should be handled by a dunning system.

 work spaces

The work spaces that you create should be as airy, light, and quiet as possible. You and others will be spending substantial amounts of time there. By making these spaces as healthy and beautiful as possible, you will add joy and greater productivity to your working hours.

Simple Pricing

Setting a price for what you make or do can be a challenge, especially if you think of yourself as mathematically inept. If that's what you think, get over it! If you can add and subtract, then common sense will help you arrive at a price that works. Pricing is not difficult if you can face it and back it up with confidence.

Recipe for a Price

A price has to work for *you* first, and then for your wholesale and/or direct retail customer. Regardless of how much time and how many dollars are needed to make and sell a product or service, if an item is priced too high it simply will not sell. And if it will not sell on the retail level for the price that you and your wholesale buyer need to achieve, then you are wasting your time, ruining your credibility, and ultimately setting yourself up for failure.

Many inexperienced marketers are so anxious to be successful that they arbitrarily lower their prices to a level that assures sales. At first it seems to be working. Sales are high, the reorders are high, and the business owner is "high" on the promise of success. The high allows them to overlook some things — namely, the huge number of hours that they are

Direct retail customer: An individual customer who purchases goods or services for personal use.

Wholesale customer: A cataloger or store owner who purchases your products to sell to their own direct retail customers.

Distributor: A large-volume customer who warehouses your products and sells them to wholesale customers.

Consignment: The practice of placing your products for sale in a store; you are paid if and when your products sell, and the store keeps a certain percentage of the sale price (usually around 40 percent).

Commission: The percentage of sales money paid to shop owners (who sell your product on consignment in their stores) or sales representatives (who sell your product to their accounts).

Sales representative: On-the-road customer service; a person who will visit existing accounts (stores that already sell your products) and potential new accounts within a particular geographic area to market, promote, and sell your products.

working, the small amount of money that they are earning for their time, and the other responsibilities in their lives that they are neglecting. They believe that if they can reach a higher level of success, they will be able to justify unpaid hard work, debt, and an unhappy family. A person intoxicated with the possibility of future success will keep telling himself or herself that everything will come out all right in the end. In fact, such persons may even be thinking that they will soon be rich and will have plenty of time and money to make up for their current shortcomings.

Sorry, friends, but this is a bad recipe! Basing a price on what the market will respond to is a great idea *only* if that price is enough to cover all the materials and time needed to remain in business over the long haul. If an item will not sell for the price that you and your wholesale customer need to get, then you have two options:

- Take less than you should, thereby setting yourself up for financial failure and personal burnout.
- Lay that particular product to rest, and concentrate on finding others that will meet your personal and financial needs over a sustained period of time.

Competition versus Camaraderie

Comrade: One that shares the same fortunes or experiences as another; a companion.

— Webster's Third New International Dictionary

Most business books will tell you to review the competition when setting your price. Because of the nature of the work we do, I think that people involved in the bodycare industry are more likely to understand the wisdom of cooperation rather than competition. And so, I would like to break with tradition by suggesting that competitors start thinking of themselves as comrades.

Comrades can call each other on the phone when they need help with a problem or an answer to a question. Competitors miss out on having each other as resources. In the past I have called for other companies' catalogs, feeling sneaky, actually, when all I wanted to do was to know what they were offering and at what price. I wanted to be certain to create new and different things. I also wanted to be certain that my prices were at least as high as the prices of others in my industry. As anyone who has attended bodycare conferences and workshops will tell you, it is always a joy to see the diversity of bodycare businesses and to gain inspiration from each other. Due to many of these conferences, I have gotten to know many of my business cohorts, and now I feel much more comfortable calling them when I need to compare notes with them.

In terms of pricing, I believe it is important for all bodycare providers to work together to keep prices as high as the market will allow. We have families and communities to feed and businesses to grow, and we need abundance to cover all of our bases. Doesn't it make sense that competition should create abundance for all, rather than knockoffs and price wars?

LEAD ON WITH THE LIGHT

Retail price: The price that you or a store owner charge a direct retail customer.

Wholesale price: The price shop owners pay you for your goods in order to sell your goods in their stores. This price does not include the cost of shipping goods to the store. Shipping costs must be added separately, and are usually paid by the wholesale customer. The wholesale price is typically half of the retail price (and sometimes less for natural food stores or co-ops).

Distributor price: The price that a distributor will pay for a bulk purchase of your product, which will then be resold to store owners. Distributor prices are usually 25 to 30 percent lower than wholesale, and you have to pay to have the goods shipped to the distributor's warehouse. The good news is that there is usually a minimum order ($1000 or more) imposed on a distributors.

Profit

The price of your product must cover all of your materials and labor, and all costs of producing, selling, or servicing your product. I use the word "all" very seriously. That means that you must consider every possible expenditure of time and money related to your entire operation. A sound price must also include what I call the "frosting" — the icing on the cake. This is your profit, the money that goes into the bank after everyone, including yourself, has been paid. The frosting is the money that is set aside for future growth and development. If your work is good, there will be an ever higher demand for your product, and you will need extra funds to keep up. So don't forget the frosting if you plan to stay in business for a long time.

Another nice thing about frosting is that it creates a sweet pool of financial resources that can be given away. Some businesspeople offer employees a share of the profits; others offer donations to important non-profit groups. "Tithing" — giving away one-tenth of the profits — is one way in which businesses can give back to the world. In fact, corporate and small-business tithing is a long-standing tradition in many economically developed countries. I feel that giving should be a planned part of every business's pricing recipe, even when the business is new — and especially if there is a great wish to be successful.

what's in a price?

Labor: Financial value placed on the time that you or someone else spends producing an item. This includes all payroll taxes, breaks, paid vacations, and sick time.

Material: All materials used to produce an item or service, including the freight costs to procure them.

Overhead: All operating costs not directly related to production. Examples include but are not limited to rent, utilities, postage, telephone, transportation, office management, bookkeeping, legal and design fees, equipment, selling expenses, and sales commissions.

Tithing: Ideally, 10 to 20 percent of your sales profits.

Profit: Ideally, 15 to 20 percent of the price should remain after all expenses and tithes have been paid.

Purchasing

Knowing how and when to purchase goods, materials, and services from other vendors is an important part of your day-to-day business decisions. You've probably heard Benjamin Franklin's wise words, "A penny saved is a penny earned." He would be welcome in my purchasing department!

Developing a purchasing system can be an art form unto itself, and there are entire chapters devoted to it in many business books. Many small businesses have a person or department whose full-time responsibility is to monitor supplies, order more before stock runs out, and maintain good relationships with vendors.

The best thing you can do for yourself and your seedling business is to seek out good sources of information. You'll want to find out who sells the supplies you'll need, what types of pricing they charge, if they service your area, if they service small businesses, and if they have a reliable business record. Do your research at the library, on the Internet, and through others in your field. Ask lots of questions, and seek out the suppliers who have the best quality, the best prices, and the best customer service, and, ideally, whose business practices support your vision of business as a force for economic and social transformation.

To get you started, examine the sample purchase order located in the appendix. A purchase order form is at the heart of all purchasing systems. It becomes a source of reference and a "check and balance" for record-keeping, receiving, accounting, and planning.

Even if you intend to delegate the details to someone else, I highly recommend that you educate yourself in the basics of purchasing. There is a very good, easy to understand chapter on purchasing in *Small Business Start Up*, by Bob Adams (see Suggested Reading for complete details).

A Philosophy of Service

*And there are those who give and know not pain
in giving, nor do they seek joy, nor give with mindfulness
of virtue; they give as in yonder valley the myrtle
breathes its fragrance into space. Through the hands
of these God speaks, and from behind their eyes
He smiles upon the Earth.*

— Kahil Gibran, *The Prophet*

Service in business is a broad topic. In the broadest sense, it encompasses the desire to live one's life in service to the greater good of all life on Earth, and to the Earth herself. In a more focused sense, it involves numerous aspects of the day-to-day life of a business. As the creator and orchestrator of your business, you'll have an unlimited number of decisions to make. The greater the love and commitment to service you are able to bring to the decision-making process, the greater your success will be. This is just my opinion, but it is based on numerous experiences and observations.

When you root yourself in the philosophy of service, you have the advantage of working from a powerful place. Decisions made within the context of this philosophy will result in a world of abundance springing up around you.

A philosophy of service is the simple act of continually asking, "How can I help? How can I help myself, my family, employees, community, and world? What can I do to make life easier and better for all of us? How can my decisions and actions make a difference?"

Business seminars and training sessions often tend to concentrate on customer service. The reason for this is that in all businesses, the key to good sales is backing up your sales with warm and genuine concern for your customers. Always deliver what you promise without delay! Once you've achieved a reputation for keeping your word, maintaining fair prices, and promptly delivering quality products, references from satisfied clients will keep your business flourishing.

The Essence of Quality

It is one thing to aspire to quality. It's a more difficult thing to deliver it on a consistent basis. A commitment to quality requires more than words to be truly meaningful. Delivering quality service or goods requires diligence! Quality-control standards, measures, and assessments must be devised and implemented. Workers must be continuously educated, inspired, and empowered to create and maintain quality.

Despite our best efforts, quality will occasionally fail. Before this happens, make sure that plans are in place for making amends to everyone who will be affected. Apologies and restitution given freely will assure you of an opportunity to maintain integrity. Integrity is the essence of quality. The two go hand in hand.

building a market

Building a market is like watering and fertilizing your garden. You've laid out the rows, planted the seeds, and now you want your garden to produce in abundance! Business in its finest form is a method for attaining abundance. But as we mentioned earlier, true abundance goes beyond money. Money, while helpful and welcome, should not be your only goal. Keep your heart open to *all* the riches available to you. Meaningful work, travel, associations with exciting new people and ideas, and opportunities for learning, giving, and personal growth await you.

Sales and Marketing

The next step in building a business and a life of abundance is to become adept at sales and marketing. While sales and marketing are related, they are not the same thing. Most successful businesspeople understand the difference.

Marketing is a system of integrated business activities: planning, designing, pricing, promoting, and distributing products and services to present and potential customers. A marketing plan or approach includes identifying the target market, creating products for that market, and then pricing, promoting, and selling those products according to the wants and needs of that market.

Sales is selling, the aspect of marketing that involves direct communication with the consumer or reseller of your product. Sales efforts involve closing the sale after interest has already been created by marketing efforts. So you have to market before you can sell. If you do your marketing well, selling will come easily. Good marketing makes selling a breeze!

Developing Products That Sell

In the past, many marketers and advertisers have focused on creating new, empty needs in people while ignoring their innate needs for love, community, health, security, and joy. As you work to develop new products and services, contemplate what people *really* need to become safer, happier, and healthier. By doing this, you will create a market for something you and others can truly believe in, as you create abundance for yourself and others.

Developing a product or service is definitely a creative art. I usually begin by seeking or experiencing an inspiration. Something that I see or do will touch my heart, and from that feeling comes an idea for sharing my heartfelt feelings with others via my business. When I develop products or services, I create a medium for sharing something meaningful, and then make it available for people to buy.

One recent example of this is the creation of a soapmakers club offered by my business. Several years ago I wrote a recipe book on soapmaking and published it through Interweave Press. Although it was one of several books published on the topic of soapmaking that year, my book was a big success, selling thirty thousand copies in the first eleven months.

All the soapmaking books that came out that year helped spawn a small niche market of hobbyist soapmakers. Many of the letters I received from happy readers commented on how much they enjoyed the poetic nature of my writing and the art of soapmaking itself. Many told me that my work had inspired them to start their own small soapmaking hobbies and businesses. I was so deeply touched that I decided to start a soapmakers club and a quarterly newsletter called *Creative Alchemy and the Poetry of Soapmaking*. The club was the first service offered by my business. We signed on nearly two hundred paid members the first year.

The club provides information and creative inspiration through networking with other soapmakers. We recently set up an Aromatic Tour of France, and a number of club members, myself included, will soon be visiting soapmakers and essential-oil distilleries and perfumeries throughout France. All of this wonderful abundance arose from the heartfelt feelings that were sent out in my book, returned to me in letters, sent out again through the soapmakers club and newsletter, and returned again via my customers in the club. I have created a wonderful pathway for giving and receiving.

Another example that comes to mind is the development of our Himalayan Goatsmilk Soap. I have been a goat keeper for many years. I have enjoyed caring for these wonderful animals since the age of twenty, and I've raised my two young sons on fresh, delicious, healthy goat's milk. I love goats!

Last year I met a woman named Pamela Carson, who had created an economic self-help project called Educate the Children (ETC) for women and children in Nepal. One of her ETC projects, Project Goat, helps fund the purchase of goats for Nepalese women by soliciting donations from people worldwide. Along with a goat, each woman also receives training in basic business, animal husbandry, health, and hygiene. When Pamela showed me how Project Goat had improved the lives of so many in Nepal, my heart was just a-humming! I wanted to tell everyone about Project Goat. So I created a design and formula for Himalayan Goatsmilk Soap. The design included a donation sheet explaining the project, which would be inserted into each package of soap. And my pricing included a tithing to Project Goat itself.

While goats and soap may not seem such an unlikely partnership, another one of my marketing projects involves wolves. When I read about the wolf restoration efforts in Wyoming's Yellowstone Park, I was truly inspired. I went to my favorite thinking rock in the middle of the St. Regis River, and designed the Wolf Restoration Soap. The label tells about wolf restoration in Yellowstone, and a portion of the proceeds from the sale of the soap is donated to the project. This cooperative project allows a moment of hope for the future that my customers can think about while they enjoy their morning shower. Today SunFeather Wolf Restoration Soap is sold in many national park gift shops and museum stores as well as the L. L. Bean store in Freeport, Maine, and to my delight, there is a wolf restoration project taking shape in my own neck of the woods — the Adirondack mountain region of New York state.

Wolves and goats were an easy inspiration and they brought immediate success. A more challenging marketing project I recently undertook involves the marriage of tobacco, soap, and the sacred. I have had this project on a back burner for a long time. Tobacco was honored for thousands of years by North American indigenous people as a sacred and powerful herb. It was used sparingly in ceremonial contexts. Native people understood that the plant was powerful and had the ability to alter one's physiology and consciousness. Within their cultural context, it also had the power to connect one with the divine.

In modern society, so separated from the gifts of nature, this herb has been grossly overused, misused, and abused for the past seventy-five years — since the advent of marketing and advertising. The social and personal health costs caused by this abuse are billions of dollars annually. The market potential for a solution to this enormous problem is equally enormous.

Based on all of this, I was inspired to create a Medicine Tobacco Soap. The packaging educates people about the original gift of tobacco, and suggests that addiction can be broken by communicating with the sacred essence of the plant and asking for release from its powerful grip. This suggestion may be a stretch for the logical Western mind, but this type of thinking is slowly gaining greater understanding as subjects like deep ecology and sacred earth philosophies emerge more fully into our collective consciousness. I love using my business to advance this type of understanding.

As I was working on the project, I was amazed to get a phone call from a woman named Lucy Harrison, from the American Indian Health and Family Services in Dearborn, Michigan. She had heard that I often tithe money to nonprofit organizations. I told her about my Medicine Tobacco Soap (in fact, I was holding the label artwork in my hand when she called). She told me that her office was currently working on a health education leaflet addressing exactly the same topic as my tobacco soap. Now, people who are attracted by the prospects of tapping into the sacred to find cooperation and strength for overcoming addiction will find Lucy's number on my soap label as well as in my catalog.

These are examples of cooperative marketing that helps society as it helps business. I suggest a "new people's network" as a timely replacement for the outdated "old boys' network." Today, we know that two cultural creative heads are better than one. Cooperative marketing can be lucrative *and* it gets us to the heartbeat and hope of life.

SEEK A BALANCE BETWEEN NATURE AND BUSINESS

Selling Made Easy

Most people do not enjoy selling. This problem often begins in grade school when students are given chocolates or trinkets to sell to raise money for the school band or some other specialty club. Parents cringe when the goods are brought home, and relatives may feel more like victims than customers. I have thought about this problem a lot and believe I have discovered a beneficial way to rethink the selling scenario.

It's really very simple. It begins with the premise that it is easy and fun to sell things you love and believe in. So if you think selling is a big black hole, think again. In order to have a healthy business, you will need to adopt a healthy attitude toward selling. By making a commitment to develop only goods and services that you believe in, you will be able to easily transcend any negative feelings about sales. When you take your good products and services to market and the market loves your creations, the selling will be as free and easy as a warm summer day.

The Helpmates: Promotion, Publicity, and Advertising

When it comes to business, promotional, publicity, and advertising materials are as important as intuition and quality! Since your business stationery, brochures, catalogs, fliers, press releases, and posters will be seen by existing and potential customers as well as publicists, they must look beautiful and professional, and they must speak meaningfully in pictures and words about your work.

⁂ *sage advice* ⁂

USE A LOGO

It's a good idea to create a theme or look for your business. A logo helps create product- and name-recognition if you consistently use it on all of your promotional materials, products, and displays.

Brochure and Catalog Design

Designing brochures and catalogs is a very creative and important task. If you cannot afford a twelve-page catalog, create a two-page catalog — but be certain that those two pages are the best that money can buy.

The same is true for brochures. A brochures is usually one sheet of paper printed on two sides and folded into halves, thirds, or quarters. Brochures are excellent tools for small companies with a limited number of products or services. A full-color brochure will cost more, but its selling power can more than make up for the money you spend on it. With the availability of desktop publishing, a professional color brochure complete with photos is attainable for even the smallest of businesses. Some may start with this option, then graduate to an offset printing job after evaluating the success of a promotional piece.

I worked with brochures for the first six years of my company's existence, before the advent of desktop publishing. I drew and lettered my first brochure by hand. I had been in business for three months selling at local fairs before I saved the $200 required to print it. It was a one-color job and had a small order form on the back. One day, lo and behold, my first wholesale order, for $12, arrived in the mail. I knew then that I was on my way!

With the vast popularity of desktop publishing and the abundant number of talented users, it should be easy to produce a wonderful brochure for very little money. If you are going it alone as far as design is concerned, either with desktop publishing or offset printing, be certain to select a print shop or publisher that is willing to work closely with you to achieve the results you desire.

In order to obtain good results, begin by visualizing and developing your brochure or catalog design. Collect selling pieces from other com-

⌐ sage advice ⌐

CASH ALTERNATIVES

If you're short on cash, consider finding a graphic designer or printer who will barter or trade with you. Offer them products or services in exchange for your work, and/or give them sizable credit on your promotional piece so that they'll benefit from the publicity you create.

panies by writing or calling them. (There are company listings in most trade show directories.) When you receive the materials, review each one and highlight the aspects that you like. Pay attention to color, shape, size, weight, design, mood, paper selection, and any other unique features.

Look at how the copy is written and laid out. Brochures have space constraints; copy must be as succinct and direct as possible. A catalog, on the other hand, offers more space. That space can be used creatively to express your business philosophy, your product or service, and yourself!

The next step is to create a mock-up brochure or catalog. This can be done on your home computer or by hand. I enjoy creating mine by hand, and I usually make a jumbo version of what I want, keeping it to scale. Using rubber cement, scissors, double-stick tape, stapler, ruler, and erasable colored pencils, I use my hands to help guide my imagined design into physical form. It helps to develop a written master list of everything you wish to include in your piece. Then imagine a sensible sequence, and assign each item a number. Your next step will be to assign a space on your mock-up to each numbered item.

Decide how large your photos, sketches, or designs will be. Sometimes it's helpful to have color photocopies made of photos or artwork, reduced to the size needed for your mock-up. Type in or hand-write your text. Placing the photocopies, type, and designs in different places, you will really begin to visualize how the finished product will look. When your mock-up takes its final form, make enough copies of it to take to several printers. These will be very useful in giving printers a clear understanding of what you want, and in helping them give you an accurate price quote for your job.

∿ *sage advice* ∿

BECOME A CREATIVE COPYWRITER

Don't neglect the copy in your catalog or brochure! Creative, well-written copy can educate and inspire. Tell about the benefits of what you offer and help to create desire for your product or service. If you don't think your writing skills are up to par, just jot down your ideas and ask a talented friend to create written copy from your ideas.

A well-designed catalog or brochure should be attractive, creative, informative, engaging, beautiful, and fun. Once you have it in your hands, you will be holding one of the most powerful selling tools ever invented. For the price of postage, it can go places that you would be unlikely to go. It can serve as a sales ambassador, traveling home with one customer who just purchased your product or service, and then perhaps passed along to another. If your catalog communicates well through words and pictures, and if you can get it into the hands of people who are likely to want what you have to offer, it will work hard for you. It can accomplish things that you could never have accomplished otherwise.

Finding Free Publicity

Creative and beautiful promotional materials are literally worth their weight in gold! By sending promotional literature, press releases, and product samples to magazine and newspaper editors, television and radio producers, resource directories, and Internet networkers, you can receive free publicity for your service or product.

A few years ago, I experimented with investing my time (about seven hours a week for eight consecutive weeks) into sending out press releases about my products along with color slides and catalogs. I also sent letters

EMBELLISHING YOUR PROMOTIONAL LITERATURE
Consider publishing your company's mission statement on your promotional literature. Photos of you and your staff will bring home the concept that your business is a small and personal one. This imparts an unspoken promise of quality and accountability, which many consumers seek.

to magazines and book publishers asking if they would like me to write about my business for them. I interested local newspapers in my work and even captured a thirty-minute feature on the local public television station. That feature is still being rerun. The immediate financial value of my effort was thousands of dollars in sales. The long-term financial value has been tens of thousands of dollars. The other types of abundance that my efforts created were immeasurable.

After the success of this experiment, it has become a standard routine in my business for someone to invest a certain amount of time every week into obtaining free publicity. If you are operating on a shoestring budget, obtaining free publicity will assure your business of an advertising budget that will cost you only time. This is time well spent!

Developing an Advertising Program

Billions of dollars have been earned and lost on advertising. It takes a certain sixth sense to be good at advertising. It also takes knowledge of the reading, listening, and viewing habits of your customers. Some companies survey their customers to discern this information while others make intuitive deductions and then test them on ad performance. In the end, it takes plain old trial and error to evolve a sound advertising program for your business.

Most business consultants recommend that a business spend between two and ten percent of its gross income on advertising. That money should be spent regularly, because it is steady, repeated advertising that brings in customers. The less you can afford an advertising campaign, the more you probably need one. Though many small businesses manage exclusively on free publicity and word of mouth, if they wish to grow, they'll eventually need to incorporate advertising into their operating budgets.

The smaller your advertising budget, the more important it is to spend wisely. Ads must be repetitive to be effective, so only advertise if you can afford to do so regularly. If your business is seasonal, you'll want to plan your advertising dates accordingly.

Advertising expenses fall into two categories: production and media. Production expenses such as typesetting, art, creative design, and layout, can be minimized if you know how to use a desktop publishing system. Broadcast production expenses include studio time, tape, design, and talent. Media costs include the purchase of time on television and radio, and space in newspapers, magazines, trade magazines, and show directories.

To help figure out the advertising venues appropriate for your business, make a list of all media appropriate to your business, such as newspapers, magazines, circulars, public access television, radio, and so on. Check your local library for *The Gale Directory of Publications, Bacon's Publicity Checker,* and *The Gebbie Press House Magazine Directory,* all good sources of information about publicity and advertising resources. The Department of Commerce also publishes a state-by-state list of trade publications. Call or write for advertisers' rate cards. Make a chart comparing geographical circulation, cost per square inch, cost for color versus black and white, copy deadlines, and run dates. Use this chart to choose your favorite advertising possibilities.

 design an advertising calendar

Make a twelve-month calendar on one large sheet of paper, or buy an erasable one that can be reused every year. Note all ad copy deadline dates, the dates the ads will run, and letter or number codes for ads. Hang this calendar on your office wall near a file filled with ad contacts, contracts, and performance evaluations.

Ad Design

The best way to begin designing printed advertising is to look carefully at the advertisements of other companies. Which ones are most noticeable and effective? A successful ad usually says a lot by saying less. An effective ad will be designed in a manner that is visually attractive to your customers, and it will have a look that your customers can relate to.

The use of color, photographs, typestyles, and art can help you achieve uniqueness and simplicity for maximum impact. Good ads have several components in common:

- A headline with a short, eye-catching phrase or question.
- A body of text that briefly explains what you're selling and why someone would want it.
- Frequent mention of your company and product by name.
- A price list, incentives, catalog offers, company logo, address, phone and fax numbers, and, if applicable, your e-mail and Web site addresses.
- An ad code that will help you identify where your orders are coming from and which advertisements are working best.

 ## the golden rules of advertising

Remember the two golden rules of advertising:

1. Always stress the advantages and benefits of the product or service you wish to sell.

2. Always put a code in the return address of your ads so that you will know which ads are working for you. For example: Sandy's Soaps, 4444 Rachel Carson Way, Dep't NH7. (This stands for the July issue of *Natural Health* magazine.) This coding system will help you to evaluate the performance of your ad.

Ad Production

Unless you are good at desktop design and have the equipment to output the film and electronic files that your advertiser will require, you'll need to find a graphic designer or ad agency to produce your ad. Most publications have ad design services. Some are costly, some are reasonable, and some are free. Be certain to shop around! In any event, you'll need to sketch a mock-up of your ad on paper. Then attach examples of other ads that you like, explaining which effects you'd like to see in your ad. Give this information to the publication, ad agency, or freelancer that will design your ad. Always proofread your ad before it is finalized. Be certain to ask for copies, paper and electronic if possible, of your final ad layout so that you can begin building a file of ads.

Once your ad is produced, you may not want to face the challenges of advertising and publicity. If so, consider hiring a publicity agency or freelancer to get the job done. By working closely with a professional ad agency or freelance advertiser, you can gain a wealth of knowledge about advertising and publicity. Systems tailored to your business will be developed and implemented, so be certain you have access to all records your advertiser creates. This way, if something goes amiss in your relationship, you will have all the data you will need to either engage a new advertiser or do the task yourself.

Direct Advertising

OK, let's face it. You're not ready to hire an ad agency. Maybe there is no money in your advertising budget. Possibly there is no budget at all, just a small fledgling company waiting to take wing. My company was like that in the beginning. But don't despair — where there is a will, there is direct advertising!

Direct advertising is a hands-on approach that is your only hope if you're too poor to advertise and too small to get publicity. It may include fliers and samples given out on the street or delivered door-to-door. It may include a demonstration or talk about your work at the monthly garden club meeting. It may mean setting out your wares on a blanket at a Phish concert!

One massage therapist I know offered to give free fifteen-minute lunchtime massages at a local factory. The response was so positive that the owner of the company hired her to come in weekly. She now offers mini workshops on health and natural healing, and has helped the company's workers become more health conscious. She has also gained a number of new customers who see her regularly for full massage sessions.

If your product or service is good, be generous about giving it away. Your generosity is sure to create a return, in more ways than one. Other low-cost direct advertising includes posters and notices on bulletin boards, on your car, and even on your pets!

One innovative New York City businesswoman put a sandwich board on her large poodle to advertise her herbal pet care products. As she and Fifi le ShampPoo walked down the street, people would request her direct mail flier. She also made it a practice to give out twenty-five free samples each day. With this type of creativity, generosity, and determination, I expect that this young woman will someday be at the helm of a highly successful pet care product business — or the CEO of her own dog walking/advertising agency.

Direct Retail Selling

In the beginning stages of a small business, it makes a lot of sense to learn about selling your service or product by selling directly to customers. This is called direct retail selling.

Many service businesses sell only at the direct retail level, though eventually they may expand into offering a product line related to their service. For example, the Finger Lakes School of Massage in Ithaca, New York, was clearly a service business in the beginning. But eventually its owners opened an aromatherapy retail store and began selling books, sheets, candles, oils, and other products related to their service. Now the store and the school create interest in each other, offering mutual support and a constant exchange of customers.

Selling at Fairs

When I began my company I relied solely on retail fairs and events to market my product line. Meeting the customers personally and learning about their likes and dislikes was a very valuable experience for me. I was also able to learn what prices attracted them and what ones turned them away.

The most important thing to know about marketing at fairs is that you need to find a few good customers and then stay with them. Educate those customers about your work, gain their loyalty, and turn them into regular visitors to your booth each year. There will always be new customers, but it is this base of regular customers that you want to nurture and expand.

Aside from the inherent pleasures of a well-planned and well-attended fair, there is a financial advantage as well. When you sell at a fair, you are selling directly to the consumer. This means you are eliminating the "middle man," namely, the shop owner who takes a 20 to 50 percent commission on consignment sales, the wholesale buyer who expects 50 percent of the retail price, or the sales representative who requires a 10 to 20 percent commission.

For your first time out, a small local fair will do. As you become more adept at booth design, producing, marketing, and selling, you'll want to branch out to attending more professional shows. Most professional shows are well-planned and publicized events. They draw large crowds, creating the potential for sales ten to twenty times greater than at a small local fair. Remember though, that your expenses will be higher as well. Often professional shows and festivals are judged months ahead of time. (*The ArtFair Sourcebook* is a good source of information about shows and evaluations of shows — see Resources.)

Direct retail selling at fairs and festivals is an excellent way to explore the fine art of selling while networking with other small-business owners. As if this is not enough, you will also gain valuable insights about your customers and products. Don't miss out!

Mail Order

Obviously, to make direct retail selling successful you need to have effective marketing and selling materials. Then it becomes a matter of generating leads, sending out sales materials, and handling sales.

One direct benefit of retail marketing at fairs is the opportunity to build a database of people who love your work. By reaching these people with periodic mailings of your catalogs, special offers, and new products, you will be able to stimulate sales without stepping a foot outside your home or office. Add to this the mailing of catalogs or brochures to rented mailing lists, and the customers who respond to your advertising and publicity, and you will soon be swooning at your mailboxes — both electronic and old-fashioned — each day. Before you know it, you will have created a vibrant retail market right from your own home!

Direct-mail marketing campaigns have been studied and practically turned into a science of probabilities. There are numerous books written on this subject, and I have listed several in the suggested reading list in the back of this book. You can also find direct-mail consultants who work on a percentage of income. If you decide to develop your own direct retail market, take the time to build slowly until you know what you are doing. Good record keeping will help you to make sound decisions as you gain experience.

 ## *mail-order rules and regulations*

The Federal Trade Commission requires truth in advertising for mail-order marketers. In addition, consumer safety and labeling laws must be followed, and all mail orders must be shipped within thirty days or the money must be refunded. Regulations pertaining to your specific field of endeavor should be researched at the library or by a lawyer before you go into business.

Selling at Home

If you have extra room in your home, you can earn money where you live. I know of many home spas, home bodycare workshops, home massage businesses, and home cosmetic and soapmaking businesses with products available for sale on site. This has the advantages of convenience, low overhead, and low risk, along with the disadvantages of diminished privacy and lack of a professional atmosphere.

Some enterprising people will organize home events during the holiday season when buying (and stress) levels are brisk. The more relaxed atmosphere of the home helps customers enjoy themselves while shopping. Home parties such as these can require a great deal of organization. Much of the planning can be patterned after the standard home-party plans of Tupperware, Pampered Chef, or any of the other popular home party opportunities. However, the time invested is worth the effort, as profit margins from home selling tend to be quite generous.

Selling Products to Stores

Store owners who buy products from you (at a discounted price) to sell them at their stores are your wholesale customers. There are several routes to selling your product line to stores. The most basic way is to put on a comfortable pair of shoes, gather up your samples, promotional materials, and order blanks, and start walking and talking. If you're a preplanner and forward thinker, you'll want to call ahead for appointments to meet with interested buyers at the best stores you can find. Be sure to space your accounts out over several blocks! Small-town stores are very conscious about having many stores selling similar products, so your best strategy is to sell only to the best stores in town.

Personalizing Account Relationships

I recently discovered the results of paying more attention to individual wholesale accounts. Since I had just moved to a new town, I took the opportunity to contact two stores that I had been selling to for many years. I had never met the owners, nor had I spoken with them on the phone. Our past history had consisted of a few mail orders a year. One was a natural food store and the other was a craft cooperative. I spent time working in both stores, giving out samples and educating people about my products.

This investment of time was valuable in several ways. I made new friends, I got to know my customers, and I learned many things from them. I also increased my sales in each store by a factor of four! Does the personal approach to selling make a difference? For me it certainly does!

Now I am trying to figure out how to extend this type of personal service to a greater number of accounts. Many would say that this is the job of a sales representative, (a person who will visit accounts and sell your product to stores within a specific geographical area). Sales reps can fulfill this role if you're too shy or too busy to sell in a highly personal, hands-on manner. Using sales reps may sound easy, but from my own experience I can assure you that it is not!

Using Sales Representatives

Sales representatives can be a perplexing lot. Often I have found them to be overworked and underpaid, moving from job to job, and not always reliable. Less often, I have found well-organized independent reps who are highly successful at what they do. What they do is sell for you. If they are really good, they will develop personal relationships with each account, much like I did with the two stores previously mentioned. In exchange, you write them a check for 10 to 20 percent of all sales to those accounts in a monthly statement.

Independent sales reps usually work a certain territory within a 200-mile radius of where they live. Repping groups (corporate organizations of sales representatives) usually have a territory of several states and hire many reps to cover various locations for them. Many repping groups have the advantage of a showroom and are able to sell for you from these showrooms as well.

Some reps cover gift and museum stores, others sell to specialty boutiques, pharmacies, natural food stores, and outdoor stores. Finding several reps who are compatible with what you do can be a challenge. Some are listed on the Internet; others advertise in trade publications; still others can be found working in showrooms and at major trade exhibitions.

The best way to find a good rep is to attend a trade exhibition as a guest or manufacturer. Look for product lines similar to yours, and you may well find a rep standing right in front of you. Seek someone who you feel compatible with. It's really a hit-or-miss type of experience. For every four that don't work out, there will be one with whom you will be able to develop a very lucrative partnership. By the way, if you preview a trade show, consider the possibility of becoming an exhibitor in the next exhibition.

Selling at Trade Shows

After you've been in business for a while you will know what sells at what price. You will know what it means to provide a service or manufacture a product. Delivery of your product or service will have become streamlined and efficient. Your income will be growing, offering you opportunities to try new things. You may decide that you want to take a leap and expand your business. Along with this comes higher sales and more employees, bigger headaches and also greater abundance.

One way to do this is to include trade shows in your marketing plan. A service business may increase its customer base by attending women's shows, garden shows, and health and fitness shows held in the area. Product manufacturers will want to consider wholesale gift shows, fashion boutiques, natural product shows, outdoor shows, salon, spa, and beauty shows.

The cost of attending these types of shows is quite high, and the financial return may not be immediate. The purpose of attending a show is to promote your business by handing out catalogs and fliers, gaining new customers, making contacts with the media, and servicing existing customers. You will write orders at shows, immediately following shows, and for a long time afterward. Therefore, plan on delayed abundance after exhibiting at a show. It will build over time.

There are many things to consider and many expenditures to make before you are ready for a show. Set a budget goal and try to work within that framework.

Preparation

An important part of preshow planning includes the preparation of fliers or catalogs to hand out at the show. These handouts can eventually reap as much as an additional 35 percent of show sales in postshow sales.

Be certain that all promotional materials are attractive, professional, and easy to understand. They should include a faxable order form, credit and payment terms, and delivery information. There are a number of excellent books listed on page 144 that go into detail about wholesale order forms and terms of business. Review these as you develop your show promotional pieces.

∽ sage advice ∾

KEEP IT FUN

Marketing through promotional material, shows, or direct contact is rewarding, fun, and exhausting! Great perseverance, stamina, and a good sense of humor are required. Not much will go according to plan, so learn to enjoy and profit from the unexpected!

Designing a Booth

Before you sign the exhibitors contract, you'll need to design and develop an attractive and portable booth. You will probably need to solicit the assistance of a woodworker, sign maker, and seamstress, so plan well in advance of your show date deadline. A simple booth checklist would include:

— a professional sign
— backdrops
— table and riser covers
— lighting
— carpet or flooring
— display props for your products

Previewing a trade show before attending it as an exhibitor will give you a chance to look at many booth design ideas, and will help you design your own booth. Enjoy using your creativity to design and build a booth with a look and feel that will be uniquely yours!

To design your booth, begin with graph paper and pencil or a computer design program. Sketch out the entire floor plan of your booth (usually 10 feet by 10 feet, or 3 meters square). Consider the feel and look that you wish to create and then make a list of everything you will need to create it. Most booths can be built with a minimum of difficulty if properly planned.

Sales and Marketing via the Internet

The Internet is new to so many people, but it is filled with great potential and possibility. Using the Internet for sales and marketing is just one facet of this amazing and powerful tool. A number of businesses (including some flower, book, and music providers) have found ways to become extremely successful on-line. Many other companies have spent thousands of dollars and are still waiting for results. Though you may or may not become a major player in electronic marketing, there is certainly a place for the Internet in your business should you wish to explore the opportunities. I have made room for it in my work life and have been pleased with the options it has offered.

I began my Internet exploration by placing my name on a listserver for soapmakers. For several months I read thousands of writings from hundreds of soapmakers. I participated in on-line chats in my field. I learned many new things, remembered many old things I had forgotten over the years, and found a great deal of inspiration. Researching suppliers became easier when I learned how to use the Thomas Registries, a database listing most U.S. suppliers, on-line. Locating other small body-care companies has become easier too, as more and more put up Web sites. Many of these companies are now linking their Web sites and sharing customers and resources.

I have involved SunFeather in a number of on-line malls and selling media and have experienced small successes in direct selling. Eventually, I believe that many of the obstacles to achieving marketing success on-line will diminish and momentum will build. I highly recommend that all serious businesspeople explore their options on the Internet and allow their understanding of it as a business tool to grow. Several Internet business resources are listed in back of this book.

EDUCATE YOURSELF

the art
of management

maintaining, growing, and sustaining your business

I look to the infinite beauty and simplicity of Nature, with its perfect forms of order and chaos, to guide the teaching in this chapter about business management.

One thing you'll notice about a garden is that abundance doesn't arise from perfect orderliness — chaos has a role as well. You can't control the onslaught of green tomato worms that devastate your crop, nor can you control the soil conditions that make it better to grow cucumbers than petunias. You can't control the amount of rainfall you'll have this summer, nor can you control the timing of the first fall frost. A successful manager will work to sustain in the garden the natural balance of cooperation between plants and environment found in the wilds, allowing room for both the order and the chaos that bring about change, refinement, and growth.

When managing your business, keep your mind open. Be aware that more often than not, challenges or failures are not the result of a lack of order, but rather the natural cooperation of chaos. Like the gardener, you must allow your business to have the flexibility to change, refine, and grow.

In preparation for writing this book, it has been interesting to read, for the first time in my life, books about business theory. Having never had the benefit (nor the hindrance) of a formal business education, I often rely on chance, natural order, intuition, and common sense to guide the evolution of my business. Ironically, my rather uninformed and nonaggressive approach to business management seems to have worked just fine!

THINK WITH YOUR HEART

If I had to name three personal strengths that have allowed my success, they would be an ability to trust and delegate, a commitment to loving kindness, and a pioneering spirit. Similarly, you will bring your own individual strengths and gifts to your business. But whatever those strengths may be, and whether you work alone or with others, your business will require you to become a leader. Every businessperson brings to this requirement a new and different approach to leadership. Some have a knack for it, while others struggle to meet the challenge. It is true that sometimes a leader is born, but more often, a leader emerges in spite of him- or herself, from the heart of many experiences.

Your business will offer you an unparalleled opportunity to engage in experiences that will teach you to lead both yourself and others. As you lead your business forward, you will aspire to inspire self-motivation and help your organization find meaning, community, dignity, and love. You will learn how to build organizational coherence, and how to best suit activities to purpose. You will learn to create, as nature does, flexible organizational structures that empower and enable, rather than inhibit growth. You will learn how to simplify. You will learn how to offer freedom and autonomy to yourself and others. Your mission will be to design an organization that is alive and instructive, one that honors, enriches, and taps into the wholeness and loyalty of everyone involved.

As with all natural systems, parts of your organization will work in perfect harmony for a time, then they will become chaotic and "fall apart" as circumstance dictates. Systems, markets, and people will always be in a state of flux and change. As an integral part of business management, you must be willing and able to embrace chaos as you adapt, and assist those around you to adapt to these changes. Management in a nutshell, then, is this: *To inspire people to achieve their personal best while functioning within a team in order to accomplish the ever-changing goals and objectives of a business.*

Become the Best Leader You Can Be

Successful business leaders use good judgment, act purposefully and confidently, are fair and consistent, communicate clearly, listen intently, respect and support their employees, create a culture of teamwork, lead by example, know what they know, and know what they don't know. This may seem like a lot to ask for, but if you'll take to heart the skills listed below and do your best to employ them in your role as leader of your business, you'll find that you've become an inspiring and motivating business leader and workforce manager.

Managerial Skills

As the "master gardener" of your business, there are a number of managerial skills you will need to cultivate. Adopt them, practice them, and become good at them!

Good Judgment

Combine inner knowing (intuition) with outer knowing (keeping abreast of reliable, tangible information). Mix the two with a large dose of common sense and a firm eye on company goals, and you have the recipe for good business judgment. Prior to making a major decision, a savvy leader will solicit the knowledge and intuition of those who will be affected by it. Once many viewpoints are synthesized, the answer becomes clearer. As a side benefit, soliciting opinions from employees, partners, and associates helps them better understand the challenges facing the business. They are likely to become more interested in solving problems, and to view the business leader as thoughtful and methodical rather than impulsive or arbitrary. This helps the leader gain their confidence.

Purpose and Confidence

A leader with a sense of purpose has a natural air of self-confidence and resolve. If you resolve to move with positive purpose and purposeful actions, you will quickly gain the support and confidence of those around you, including your employees, customers, and financial supporters.

Fairness and Consistency

Make every effort to be fair and consistent in your actions and communications. Nothing inspires doubts and a poor reputation like inconsistencies in policies and approaches. Conversely, nothing inspires good faith and an excellent reputation like absolute fairness and consistency.

Communication and Listening Skills

Cultivate strong listening, reflecting, and positive communication skills. These skills help to troubleshoot problems, educate you and those around you toward higher functioning, and in general uplift your organization.

Respect for Employees

Wise managers choose talented people to work with. They respect their employees and support them in both their personal and their professional growth.

Teamwork

Promote teamwork within your organization as seriously as you promote the company itself. Teach it, expect it, and refuse to live without it. If you aren't skilled at building teams, learn to be, or find and hire someone who is.

Leadership by Example

Practice what you preach. Ask no more of others than what you yourself are willing to do.

Knowledge of Strengths and Limitations

By acknowledging your own strengths, you help others to identify and celebrate theirs. By knowing your own limitations, you can choose to work with people whose strengths balance out your weaknesses.

⌁ sage advice ⌁

INVOLVE YOUR FRIENDS

When SunFeather had but one employee — me — I solicited opinions from friends and family members whenever there was a big decision to be made. By setting up an informal network of advisers, I was able to tap the genius and capture the support of those closest to me.

Managerial Duties

As a leader, you will be faced each and every day with tasks that require the application of the managerial skills listed above. These are the times to practice what you've learned! Listen with an ear toward which role(s) you need to assume for each situation, and practice becoming the person you need to be for every conversation, meeting, and decision.

Visionary and Creator

A business needs creativity and vision both to be born and to stay alive. Strive to envision the future and then find creative ways to bring that vision to life in an ongoing, action-oriented way.

Planner and Organizer

Ideas are brought to life with careful planning and the organization of human and other resources. To keep your business running, you must initiate planning, organize resources, and then monitor progress.

Problem Solver

You will regularly be asked to wade through and find solutions to the inevitable challenges that businesses face.

Evaluator

You must be ready to evaluate each situation, and to act upon new information as quickly as possible.

Nurturer

Learn to adopt the role of nurturer in your relationships with customers, employees, vendors, media, and salespeople. Through example, you teach others in the organization to do the same.

Communicator

Keep the lines of communication open, honest, and clear with and between employees, customers, professional associates, and vendors.

Coordinator

Think of your business as an orchestra with many different instruments that must work together, and then orchestrate the various players in order to create harmony.

Building an Ethical Business

What does it mean to be an ethical businessperson? What does a socially responsible business look like? Is it possible to integrate social responsibility into a small company's mission and operations? These questions are important ones: They are questions about our collective future and what we wish to make of it.

On the package of my New Millennium soap/shampoo bar, created in 1996, I wrote, "The thoughts and actions of the past have created the present, and the thoughts and actions of the present shall create the future. May our future be one of peace, harmony, and plenty." This seems like a simple enough concept. But how can we earthlings evolve beyond what seems to be no longer working toward a sustainable and positive future? The answer lies in changing the way we think and act!

The Future Lies in Ethics

Throughout this book, I have suggested that a business is akin to a garden — a small ecological system. I make this analogy because it is my greatest hope that all businesses will someday either evolve into sustainable ecological centers with both an economic and a social purpose, or that they will cease to exist.

These days, business has a lot of influence on and is influenced by the way we collectively think and act as a species. Due to the fact that goods, services, and products from every country are available in almost every other country, that advertising spans the globe, and that less developed nations are aspiring to attain greater levels of development, it seems obvious that business is a worldwide medium of human endeavor and communication — for better or for worse.

What are the trendsetting, cutting-edge business philosophers talking about these days? They are talking about the future of business — and of life itself — in terms of social and ethical responsibility. Take, for example, the International Society for Ecological Economics (ISEE). With members from business communities in more than eighty countries on six continents, ISEE's philosophy centers around the marriage of ecology and economics. "Ecological economics" is a cross-disciplinary field. It reaches beyond traditional economic concepts and attempts to integrate many different perspectives in order to achieve a world that is both ecologically and economically sustainable. ISEE leaders simply state, "In the end, a healthy economy can exist only in symbiosis with a healthy ecological system."

Another example of cutting-edge business philosophy is the Global Futures Foundation, a nonprofit organization working together with businesses to explore opportunities for profit, innovation, and sustainability through the emulation of natural systems.

In the wake of corporate conglomerates, third-world exploitation, overpaid CEOs, worldwide pollution, devastation of natural resources, and other irresponsible business practices, it is refreshing to know that remedial trends are on the horizon.

These trends are evidenced as business leaders incorporate new thoughts and visions of social responsibility into their daily agendas. Ethical business practices are the starting point from which we as businesspeople can begin to effect worldwide change in the "business as usual" mindset. By walking our ethical talk, we help pioneer the evolution of business into something that is vibrant, sustainable, and alive for myriad good reasons.

There are numerous other organizations, conferences, books, and publications focusing on the development of ethics and social responsibility as a sweeping trend in business. Many are listed in the back of this book.

Responsibility Begins at Home

It does not matter how large or small your business is. What matters is that you are changing the way people view and act in the world by viewing and acting in it differently yourself.

Business for Social Responsibility (BSR), a nonprofit organization serving the needs of socially responsible businesses, offers a few suggestions on how to do this in its "starter kit," which is available to all who join BSR:

- **Create a social mission statement** that details your "positive purpose." The purposes of most socially responsible companies extend beyond the scope of earning profits. Many include as a purpose creating positive experiences and values for all stakeholders, including owners, shareholders, employees, customers, vendors, communities, and the environment.
- **Promote ethical values** that you and your company can refer to in all decision-making processes. Some of my favorites are honesty, loyalty, fairness, respect for others, compassion, and integrity.

- **Assess your performance and commitment** to your mission and ethics on a yearly basis. Share the assessment process and the findings with your employees.
- **Establish environmental principles and standards** appropriate to your business. Establish ethics versus economy guidelines for purchasing, shipping, and office practices. Use your purchasing dollars to encourage other companies to become more responsible. Inspire employees to participate.
- **Minimize waste** by creating an ethic of reuse and recycling. Check the yellow pages for resource recovery and proper waste management partners located in your community.
- **Prevent pollution** by minimizing your use of toxins, and by using an environmentally oriented print shop. Use electronic communication whenever possible.
- **Encourage energy and water conservation** in all areas of your business.
- **Design with green in mind!** Design new products, work spaces, and buildings in an environmentally conscious manner.
- **Create a friendly environment** by promoting diversity in the workplace. Create strong antidiscrimination and sexual harassment policies. Promote career and personal development. Empower employees to make decisions within the realm of their work.
- **Compensate employees** with profit sharing, stock incentives, and retirement programs.
- **Create a family-friendly business** by offering flexible hours and time off for family needs.

∿ *sage advice* ∿

LISTEN TO EMPLOYEES' NEEDS

Employees at my business, SunFeather Natural Soap Company, used to have paid vacation, sick, and personal days. But recently, we've adopted a blanket policy of "PTO" (paid time off), a personal account of time off with pay, which can be used for any reason. Employees really appreciate the increased autonomy and flexibility in scheduling their time off.

- **Promote health, safety, and wellness** through education, health insurance programs, and safe workplace policies.
- **Involve your business in the community** through local investments, training local people, and networking with local schools and institutions. Promote volunteerism by educating employees about existing volunteer possibilities, and allowing time off for volunteerism. Your managers can help with community projects, and your business resources can be used to help accomplish important community tasks.
- **Initiate philanthropy** by donating products, services, and money to community organizations and nonprofit agencies. Encourage employees to do the same by matching their donations.
- **Be an honest and positive influence in the marketplace** by making sure your claims are accurate and fair. Avoid advertising that promotes instant gratification, violence, unhealthy body image, or sexism. Demonstrate positive role models and healthy habits in advertising. Don't use advertising to exploit children. Seek marketing opportunities involving worthy causes.
- **Consider human rights at home and abroad** in your purchasing and labor decisions. Seek business associates who demonstrate concern for the fair treatment of workers.

Whether your business is a one-person show or employs many, you can make a difference in the world by setting an example of ethical behavior and thoughtful action. By organizing and managing your business around these philosophies, you will create a livelihood with meaning, purpose, and value for yourself and others.

Even though there was little written about socially responsible businesses when I began my company two decades ago, my common sense and personal sensibilities led me in that direction. After ten years adrift on a seemingly lonely sea, I finally began to see organizations, books, and articles expounding upon the new principals of business ethics, corporate responsibility, and ecological economics. I hadn't really been alone on the sea for ten years! Others were responding to the call too. It just took time to build into something highly visible. Today, thanks to a grassroots educational effort, it has become so visible that even Fortune 500 corporations are taking notice of and acting upon ideas that they wished to have nothing to do with twenty years ago. Why? Perhaps because they too are recognizing that it is in their own best interests for the world to be a safer and happier place for everyone.

Meeting Your Needs

Any business, regardless of its size, will always be a needy creature. This is especially true during its initial start-up phase. As manager and leader of your company, you must become adept at supplying whatever your business needs. Besides labor, the most common needs of a business revolve around information and finance.

Good information is crucial to good decision making and integral to creative thinking. Fortunately, informational needs are fairly easy to meet. Good managers will develop a library of information and a host of information resources that will often enable them to find needed information on their own. But at times, when highly specific knowledge is needed quickly, such as advanced legal or financial advice, the best way to get that specialized information may be to buy it. That requires the ability to work with professional accountants, lawyers, graphic designers, or business consultants. It may also require a lot of money. So, before you turn to a professional business adviser, consider your financial situation.

 for everything there is a season

Many people have a hard time accepting the possibility that their idea and their ability to advance the idea is just *not going to work*. If you've spent a year or more developing your business and things don't seem to be working *at all*, then you must reevaluate and seriously consider getting out!

Creating a Pleasant Relationship with Money

A pleasant relationship with money is built on knowledge, a positive attitude, experience, and most of all, borrowing and spending thoughtfully and carefully. Most business books seem to assume that you know enough about your business to instantly acquire a large sum of money that you will magically know exactly how to spend in the wisest manner possible. So wisely, in fact, that you'll soon be able to pay back all borrowed money without taking on three new jobs.

The sad truth is that there are many people who become captivated by the thought of starting a business. Oh, the freedom, the glory, and the boundless riches! They see other people successfully engaged in a type of lifestyle and livelihood that appeals to them. Often, they are only seeing the end result of someone else's years of hard work and utter diligence.

They want what they see, and they do what they can to get start-up money. They may get a second mortgage, borrow a large business loan from a bank or family member, or run up credit card debts. The problem is that for those who are not experienced businesspeople, chances of failure are greater than 80 percent. The endings to such stories are often not happy ones. Many people spend years repaying debt incurred to start up a business that they were not prepared to run. The resulting devastation to a person's life and adventuresome spirit is a sad thing to witness.

Does this mean that you should close this book and discreetly find the nearest woodstove to toss it into? I hope not! I would rather advise you to start very small with your new business and only spend the amount of money that you can afford to lose on starting it up. Start small, go slowly, and learn as you go. When your business shows signs of success, become just a bit bolder. Build slowly and carefully. Maintain your regular outside employment for as many years as it takes to safely create a full-time paid position for yourself in your own business. Learn how to manage the finances of your business and reinvest the earnings carefully so that you can continue to build and profit. This is a sane and safe approach for all but the most seasoned and experienced businessperson.

By playing it smart and safe, you will develop a pleasant relationship with money that will carry you where you wish to go. When you get there, you will discover that you've acquired sufficient knowledge and opportunities to fund the next stage of your company's growth.

Working with Professional Business Advisers

While I am sure that my lack of formal business education has caused me to learn lessons the hard way, I also feel it has allowed me to learn through real-world experiences. Because I haven't had exposure to what is taught in business school, I have learned to surround myself with the expertise of others.

— Diane de la Garrigue, Owner, Montage Skin and Body Studio, Redondo Beach, California

Lawyers, accountants, financial planners, graphic designers, sales and marketing consultants, advertising agencies, safety specialists, money lenders — there are lots of specialists out there! While it's always tempting to think that someone "out there" has better answers to your questions than you do, the truth is that sometimes professionals do have better answers, and sometimes they don't. If you hand over your seniority to a specialist and ignore your own inner knowing, you may end up with less than what you started with. On several occasions, I have sought professional advice, paid dearly for it, and then tossed it in the wastebasket. I've learned that if you don't have a sense of humor, you shouldn't get involved with professionals.

On the other hand, in the early stages of a business it is always a good idea to get some basic advice from an accountant and a lawyer. I didn't, and eventually paid for it with an inadequate accounting system. Your accounting system is the backbone of almost all your business decisions, so a professional approach to this is extremely important. Staying out of legal trouble is another priority. Running ideas by a lawyer who understands that you have very limited funds provides you with a basic service that will keep you out of hot water.

In choosing the advisers who will be best for your business, there are several questions you should answer. Does this professional have experience in the areas where you need assistance? Can he or she provide references? Can you afford the services of this professional? Do you feel respected and comfortable in his or her company?

It's easy to become vulnerable and hand your decision-making power over to "professionals" if you don't see yourself as one. Be sure to spell out your needs clearly, and know exactly what it will cost to fulfill those needs — or you may end up with more information (and more bills!) than you ever thought possible.

Working with Employees

As a young woman I was always pulling together groups
of people into some creative team effort. From simple
study groups to more complex endeavors, I was constantly
creating something, and yet rarely creating "alone." Now
that I have owned and operated my own business for many
years, I realize that my affinity for group effort is a kind
of entrepreneurialism in action. While many people think
of entrepreneurs as independents who "go it alone," I believe
that the most successful entrepreneurs are those who can
envision a business, and then surround themselves with
capable people to actualize it.

— Kaila Westerman, Founder/Owner,
KTB Trading, Oakland, California

The time may come when your business creates more work than you
alone can possibly do. You will try not to notice that you are working
sixteen-hour days, but eventually the light will dawn on your weary soul,
and you'll realize that you need *help!*

The degree to which business owners resist the idea of signing on
employees always amazes me. Their fears are often the same — extra
paperwork, financial responsibility, boss–employee relationships. There
seems to be a distinct lack of understanding and confidence in the hearts
of start-up business owners when it comes to hiring help. That will never
do! Everything you need to know to ease your concerns can be found in
the following pages. But first, let's replace fear and ambivalence with the
following affirmations:

- I can find a pleasant, intelligent, hardworking, and affordable
  person to help me.
- I can find someone who will be happy with a flexible schedule
  until my business can support a full-time position.
- I can find a payroll service that will ease my federal form phobia.

- When I find the right person, that person's contributions will more than pay for themselves.
- Even if, at first, I must pay my employee instead of myself, I will realize that I am building my business.

Affirmations: Positive things you tell yourself over and over again until you believe them deep within.

Next, let's document your needs.

1. Make a list of every single job that needs to be done each week to keep your business going. Assign the approximate number of hours that should be devoted to each of these tasks per week.

2. Go through the list and highlight those jobs that you do not enjoy or are not good at.

3. Separate your list into two lists: one with the highlighted jobs, and the other with all your favorite jobs.

4. Make a third list of any other jobs that you don't currently have time to do, but that you know would help your business if you could only get them done. Add the estimated number of hours per week required for each.

5. Now break up the third list and assign chosen parts of it to your job list and the remaining parts to the other job list.

6. Finally, add up the number of approximate hours for each job description. Adjust the descriptions to match the number of hours that you wish to employ yourself and your employee.

As soon as you have a job profile, you can begin to seek the perfect person to fill it.

Finding the Perfect Person

It takes time and patience to conduct a thorough search for the right employee. But remember that the person you hire may become an important part of your business and your life for years to come. So take your time! Advertise the position via word of mouth, local newspapers, and community bulletin boards. I usually ask applicants to send a résumé with references. I do not publish the name of my business or my phone number — lots of phone calls and a steady stream of job seekers can easily disrupt your workday.

I have also found good candidates through the local unemployment office. The job counselor there has already met and screened various people, and can often recommend a candidate with the skills you need. Existing employees can be a good source of ideas too. Kelly, the office manager at SunFeather, went to school with a number of our employees. She also worked with a number of them in a slipper factory years ago. She intrinsically knew which people would work out and which ones wouldn't. When I realized that Kelly's hires in the production department were much more successful than mine, I invested her with the authority to hire. Now we have four department teams and each team leader is responsible for hiring people in his or her own department.

Occasionally, if I notice an outstanding employee in a restaurant or store — someone who goes the extra mile and has a very pleasant demeanor — I give that person a notice about a job opening that I have available and encourage him or her to apply. When I write up a job description, I also include an honest description of working conditions and company policies. Many good people will want to work for you because they support your company mission, and your commitment to employee-friendly practices.

Once you have a dozen or more résumés, you can begin to screen out any inappropriate applicants. The courtesy of a letter or phone call to these people is professional must. Schedule interviews with the remaining applicants. Allow forty-five minutes for each interview and try to schedule them all over the course of two days.

 ask the universe

Throughout the history of my business, there have been times when I really needed help. My response was to make a clear plea for help to the universe. The universe has never disappointed me. It has always given me exactly what I needed when I needed it. Never discount the possibility of calling up that big employment agency in the sky to ask for the perfect employee. One will be certain to appear!

The Interview

Begin the interview by giving applicants a quick tour of your business, so that they have a sense of what you do. Offer a cup of tea to set them at ease before the formal interview begins. Ask as many direct questions as you can and listen carefully to the candidates' replies. Find out about their knowledge and experience, their interest level in the job, and their ability to perform it. How do they feel about the hours? The company's growth? Do they have any unfulfilled, burning desires that may be incompatible with your needs? I usually ask people if they have a major dream or goal in their life. The more the applicants talk the more you will learn about them.

End the interview by stating that if a job offer is extended and the applicant accepts, he or she must agree to a four-week trial period. Some companies require new employees to sign noncompete agreements (these agreements are usually drafted by lawyers), which prevent them from taking what they learn in your business and using it in a competing context away from your business.

Throughout the process of "finding the perfect person," trust your instincts as well as your intelligence. Take notes on each candidate and check the references of all your top choices. Choosing the right person for the job helps to ensure the future success of your business. The wrong person wastes time and resources, and adds undue stress to your life.

Compensation

What you pay and how you pay employees is not as difficult as it may seem. The following tips can help simplify things.

1. Job out your payroll to your accountant or a payroll service. Shop around for the best service at the best price. The time and aggravation saved by not performing the mundane tasks of calculating payroll checks and quarterly tax forms will more than cover the cost of having it done for you. Wouldn't it be nice to have all of your quarterly federal forms filed correctly and on time?

2. Consult with your accountant to determine how much you can afford to pay your new employee. Accountants will take into consideration the additional costs of payroll taxes, insurance, and other incidental costs associated with having an employee. They can also advise you about proper insurance coverage and the best place to get it.

3. If you cannot afford high salaries to attract highly competent people, then attract them with your vision of the business's future, employee-friendly working conditions, and possible profit sharing. Your accountant can advise you on ways to develop a simple profit sharing program.

Hiring: Qualities to look for include ample experience and a high interest level in the job. Applicants should have a positive, assertive attitude, a pleasant demeanor, reliable transportation, and a functional family life. They should be at ease, well organized, neat, and professional looking. They should not talk too much, not complain about previous or current employers, and should plan to give their current employer adequate notice.

Firing: If things start to feel wrong and you find yourself with an indifferent, difficult, or untalented employee, cut your losses as soon as possible and let the employee go. Be kind to employees, but not at the expense of your own happiness, or your company's reputation and profits. Be sure to first research the legalities of firing with your lawyer or local library; laws differ from state to state.

Training and Supervising

Training takes time, repetition, guidance, praise, correction, and more time. Invest as much time as it takes to help a person grasp the many aspects of a new job. Work with new hires all day at first, focusing on one thing at a time. Avoid phone interruptions so that you can offer your new employees your full attention. If they do well, praise them and yourself! If they aren't doing it quite right, say so and give them time to improve. Always be kind, patient, and straightforward. Some people are slower to learn than others, but that is not necessarily an indicator of their future worth as employees. Be patient. Offer reading and training materials if available. Ask them to feel free to solicit your help at any time. Reduce the number of hours that you work with a new hire each day, until your training objectives have been fulfilled.

Some people may continue to come back to you for assurance and support long after they should be making their own decisions. If this happens, just start asking them "What do *you* think the answer is?" Or, "How do *you* propose that we handle this one?" These types of comments will wean them away from your help, and encourage them to think and act on their own. The most important message to give your employees is that you hired them because you had faith in their ability to do a good job.

Once they learn the basics of the job, stand back and give them the freedom to do it their own way. Trust that they will pleasantly surprise you! If you have successfully trained a good employee, your job will eventually become supervisory: checking in on a regular basis, offering praise, and getting and giving feedback.

As time goes on and your business needs change, it is important to continually educate yourself and your employees through training seminars, videos, and written materials. Some jobs may outgrow the abilities of an employee to perform them and, in turn, some employees may outgrow their job descriptions. It is your job to ascertain and fulfill the ever-changing needs of your company in whatever ways you deem appropriate.

Delegating Responsibility

Once you have delegated tasks and the authority to get tasks done, allow your key employees to run things in your absence for short periods of time. This is a good exercise for both them and you — they feel empowered and you feel liberated! Delegating responsibility will teach your workers to trust themselves and you to trust your workers.

Team Meetings

Set aside at least an hour each week for a team meeting, in which your employees inform one another about the current situation. It's a good time to review and solve problems, learn from past mistakes, develop new policies, and drop outdated ones. Solicit opinions from everyone — especially the less vocal types.

◆ *sage advice* ◆

TIPS FOR GOOD RELATIONSHIPS WITH EMPLOYEES
Publicly praise good work.
Make expectations clear.
Discuss problems and give criticism privately.
Actively solicit opinions and ideas, and respect differences of opinion.
Keep written job descriptions up-to-date and challenging.
Keep employees informed about all decisions you make.
Promote from within whenever possible.
Be honest, consistent, and fair.

Finding and Keeping a Balance

*It took five years for me to launch my wholesale business.
I worked three different jobs, did craft shows on the
weekends, and hosted home parties several evenings a week.
Having no seed money made it very challenging
to build a successful business. But I did it! This is my
eighteenth year in business!*

— Nancy M. Booth, Owner, Gingham 'n
Spice, Ltd., Doylestown, PA

Many start-up entrepreneurs become completely captivated by their quest for success. Their passion allows them to summon up incredible amounts of personal energy with which they fuel the early stages of their company's growth. Many hold down a full-time job while building their company. This is no easy task!

Speaking from my own experience, the start-up phase can be both exhilarating and exhausting. But it's fun to work from a place of passion! It may be the first time in your life that you wake up in the morning so eager to get to work that you skip breakfast. Lunch whizzes by unnoticed. Supper arrives in the form of a delivered pizza. Weeks and months go by. Your personal relationships and your health are off-kilter. You work all day, all evening, and all weekend. You're on the road selling. The week before you leave is stressful, and you return to a backlog of work that has piled up in your absence. Family life has taken a backseat to your business, and what's worse, you don't care. Is there a way to launch and sustain a business without tempting this type of fate? Yes! But it requires wisdom, discipline, and planning.

Plan on devoting a tough year or two to your start-up phase. If possible, select a time in your life that will be compatible with long hours and focused work — such as before having children or after they've grown up, between relationships, or between jobs that require a great deal of your energy. I know a number of people who strategically took "no brainer" evening jobs so they could reserve their most productive working hours for the start-up phase of their business

During your start-up phase, work regular "downtime" into your schedule. Adopt an exercise plan and pay attention to healthy eating. There will be lots of excitement and lots of stress wearing on your system. Managing it well means the difference between personal success and failure.

Once your business reaches a stage where it can support at least one employee competent enough to relieve you of many day-to-day duties, back off for a while. Stay involved, but limit the number of hours you work. Use the extra time to replenish and enrich yourself with activities totally unrelated to business.

The only way to build a business from the ground up is over time. So if you're planning to be in it for the long haul, you have to pace yourself. It is helpful to remember that it is the enrichment of yourself and others along the way, not the end of the journey, that is the most important thing.

Prosperity and Abundance

The first peace, which is the most important,
is that which comes within the souls of people when
they realize their relationship, their oneness with the
universe and all its powers.

— Black Elk

The business that you have or wish to have is a powerfully creative tool. The writings that follow are about manifesting prosperity and abundance through your business. They are heart-to-heart talks about how you and your business can collaborate with universal principles and knowledge to realize personal and collective desires. Religious and spiritual traditions throughout history have often shared a similar essence in their teachings, and it is this common essence of principles and knowledge that has become known in our time as universal wisdom. If you have the inspiration to do so, you and your business can become cocreators with this universal wisdom, which is pure, simple, and available to anyone who wishes to engage it.

seek balance

If your life feels out of balance because of your strong commitment to your business, try the following telltale exercise. List the following areas of your life: work, family relationships, friendships, recreation, self-enrichment, and service to others. Estimate the number of hours per week you spend on each of these areas. Look to see where your life is out of balance. Purposefully plan to even up the scores.

Since so many of the decision-making and trailblazing abilities that I utilize in the day-to-day management of my business are of an esoteric nature, and since I have not found much written on this topic in business manuals, I feel that I should explore it in a bit of detail. If your technical business skills aren't strong, or you feel that you've never been able to do anything right in your entire life, then developing a conscious and positive relationship with the universe is your best hope.

Simple Truths

Whether you subscribe to the views of Christianity, Judaism, Islam, Buddhism, Hinduism, Wicca, Agnosticism, or any other spiritual doctrine, you will profit from a review of these universal truths:

1. Your outer world is a reflection of your deepest inner beliefs. If you aren't happy with what you have, change the way you think.

2. Abundance in the physical world is a manifestation of your *prosperity consciousness,* or your deepest beliefs about prosperity, including both your attitude toward having prosperity, your belief that prosperity is already a part of your life, and your belief that prosperity will become a bigger part of your life. So work from within. The higher your prosperity consciousness, the greater your prosperity.

3. Acknowledge the spirit within as the source of all abundance and always offer thanksgiving and gratitude for what you are given. A thankful heart is a prosperous heart.

4. Let universal wisdom and prosperity flow to you freely. When meditating or praying, do not constrict the wisdom by specifically outlining what you want. It's much better to ask for the highest possible good for your situation, and then let the universe surprise you with its infinite and abundant wisdom.

5. As your prosperity begins to mount, step back and remember that it is the divine essence that is fulfilling your journey; you are but a channel for its outpouring. The self-important mind is one of poverty. The humble mind is one of abundance.

6. Work each day to replace fearful thoughts of scarcity with confident thoughts of abundance. Focus on what is wise, true, and noble.

7. When abundance and prosperity appear, give some away to be used for the highest possible good. Remember that prosperity and abundance can be shared in many different ways besides material wealth, including teaching, loving, and providing opportunities for others.

Prosperity and Thanksgiving Exercise

If you would like to shift your consciousness and your outer experience toward greater prosperity, try the following exercises, which have been given to many woman by Iroquois medicine teacher AmyLee. AmyLee, the last initiate in a lineage of Iroquois medicine women, reminds us of the abundance that surrounds us. There are no shortages, merely blockages. To help dissolve a blockage between prosperity and oneself, AmyLee offers the following affirmation. Repeat it often throughout a day, for as long as it takes to embed itself in your consciousness. It is important to use *all* the pronouns and to keep it in the present tense. It is also important to specify what type of abundance you are seeking (financial, spiritual, social). Most important, the intent to share one's wealth gratefully is the only conscious way to approach this affirmation.

Recite or write the following three times in a row each day until you receive the prosperity that you need. *Nyahweh* (pronounced nah-way), the close of each affirmation, means "thank you."

"I, *[your name]*, do hereby attract the *[type of]* abundance of the limitless omniverse to me, *[your name]*, with gratitude and the pledge to use it wisely. Nyahweh.

"You, *[your name]*, do hereby attract the *[type of]* abundance of the limitless omniverse to me, *[your name]*, with gratitude and the pledge to use it wisely. Nyahweh.

"You, *[your name]*, do hereby attract the *[type of]* abundance of the limitless omniverse to you, *[your name]*, with gratitude and the pledge to use it wisely. Nyahweh."

Continue, using in turn the pronouns she/her, he/him, we/us, they/them. Repeat in this manner two more times.

A mind conscious of its own free will and its interrelationship with the cocreative universes realizes that what it sees (envisions, believes, and acts upon) is what it gets.

I am at my best on a creative level if I have a chance to get away from the immediate situation so that I have space to think. I enjoy exercising outdoors and I usually start my day with a four-mile run. During this time I think about whatever it is I need to figure out. Sometimes I identify what I want to know and let it simmer in the background of my mind. "Pictures" float by later on as ideas. The more I become involved in the day-to-day aspects of my business, the more my ideas come from an intuitive level. . . .

In the midst of much growth I want desperately to increase batch sizes, redo the molds, cutters, and production methods. Somewhere new products are lurking, soon to be developed. I need to find some good employees too. I am relying on faith, guardian angels, stubborn perseverance, and an intuitive belief that I can do this!

— Gretchen, Owner, Falls Creek Soap Works

Thanksgiving Exercise

If you would like a formal way to be thankful every day, here is a nondenominational prayer that anyone can use. Try to recite it outdoors whenever possible.

"Thank you, universe, seen and unseen, for all the blessings in my life. Thank you, Earth, for all that you offer so freely to assure my health and comfort."

Now face east and say: "To the powers of the east — inspiration and creativity — I send my thanks. I ask that you live within me, so that I may fulfill my purpose for the highest possible good."

Now face south and say: "To the powers of the south — faith, trust, and knowing — I send my thanks. I ask that you live within me, so that I may fulfill my purpose for the highest possible good."

Now face west and say: "To the powers of the west — goals, achievements, and dreams — I send my thanks. I ask that you live within me, so that I may fulfill my purpose for the highest possible good."

Now face north and say: "To the powers of the north — wisdom and strength — I send my thanks. I ask that you live within me, so that I may fulfill my purpose for the highest possible good."

Now face the sky and say: "Thank you sun, air, moon, and stars. Thank you, plants and trees, animals, fliers, swimmers, and crawlers."

Now face the earth and say "May I walk in balance upon this most beautiful earth." Then touch the earth with your hands.

Natural Bodycare Business Owners Speak about Inner Wisdom, Prosperity, and Divinity in Their Work Lives

During the Harmonic Convergence in August 1987, a time designated as heralding a new spiritual reawakening for all humanity, I was meditating on a remote hilltop near my farmhouse. A vision appeared to me of a symbol which eventually became WiseWays Herbals' logo. My logo's image of Isis represents healing through the use of love, compassion, and herbs, encouraging spiritual regeneration and the perfection of the divinity within.

Later that year some special friends made me a gemstone necklace with the image of my logo. After receiving the gift I had a very clear and powerful dream about creating DETOX, the first herbal inner cleansing product for WiseWays Herbals. DETOX was instrumental in the success of my business. It is still our best-seller today!

One important thing that my business has taught me is a strong belief in the presence of God/Goddess, even in the business world. That presence is flowing, driving, nurturing, and supporting us as we grow step by step. I believe that my success has been in part due to the courage I've had to express my spiritual philosophy as part of the reason for my company to exist.

— Mariam Massaro, Owner of WiseWays Herbals

As a self-employed person, my inner voice seems to be more engaged in my daily work, and I rely on it frequently to encourage me and to come up with creative solutions, as well as to give a simple thumbs up or down as I make decisions. I feel more confident in my decision-making process because I've checked in with a part of me that always has my best interests at heart.

— Kaila Westerman, Owner and founder of TKB Trading

*Do not focus too much on how a situation will mechanically work itself out.
Doing so limits the infinite number of ways that a situation can resolve itself.
Sometimes allowing a process to unfold results in something great and exciting
happening.*

— Karl Halpert, Owner, Aunt Bee's Skin Care

*I have learned to open the door to the Creator, 'cause you can't go it alone. I feel
that my spiritual, mental, physical, and emotional state of mind needs to be
gauged in some way so I can stay centered. When my mind is doing all the "talking," I can't hear the Spirit. Meditation and prayer opens me up to the spirit of
this place, the buffalo, and other helpers. It's not something that can really be
described, only experienced.*

— Bruce Gillette, Arikara/Hidatsa Native and
co-owner, Beaver Creek Company

Many business owners like these are incorporating their spiritual lives
into their work lives and finding the ultimate in satisfaction. The beautiful planet that we live on offers us abundance, prosperity, and ease. By
observing our beautiful planetary mother, we learn that scarcity is a
human-made concept. Abundance, on the other hand, is our natural
birthright. In all our human endeavors, may we aspire to cocreate this
essential right of equitable prosperity for all life.

hopes for the *future*

Consider, if you will, the far-reaching possibilities for natural businesses in the twenty-first century. The following ideas for your consideration are not solely my own. I have read about them in many current writings on topics such as ecological commerce, biopolitics, and new-wave business philosophies. These ideas have been on the frontier of new thought for a short number of years. I have watched them grow from tiny seeds to dramatic expansions of thought and vision.

It is very interesting and comforting to me that many of these writings are based in the wisdom of recent revolutionary scientific discoveries in quantum physics, chaos theory, and biology. These new discoveries are overturning the repressive models of science that have defined culture for centuries. Based upon the truths of the "new science" it seems likely that people will no longer be able to honestly view the world in reductionist terms where measurable physical reality is the only reality. Soon, I believe, the general population will adopt and acknowledge the incredible power of the human being to co-create with natural forces, to heal and uplift what has heretofore gone asunder.

As new science informs our worldview, we are offered insights from the living patterns of subatomic nature. These insights, no doubt, shall eventually transform how we organize our work, our biological and social communities, and ourselves. We are left with many hopes and questions for the future.

What will happen . . .

. . . when business becomes a positive role model for other institutions and segments of society?

When customers, employees, and onlookers witness and experience a values-driven business, it inspires the best in them. When people see and experience goodness, generosity, and healing in action it generates hope, and hope inspires additional positive change. This has already begun.

... when small business responds to the moral need for democratization of the international economic order and supports its implementation?

As more people become aware that each and every living entity on our planet deserves an equitable chance for comfort and survival, consumers will begin to scrutinize their purchases. Thousands of frivolous consumer items and foods available in today's marketplace will be viewed as wasteful and detrimental to health and happiness, and these items will surely fall away from view. As more and more businesses educate consumers about earth-friendly and people-friendly choices, consumers will demand that their buying power be utilized to enhance the future, not threaten it. This has already begun.

... when business actively advocates a "living economy" in which human and natural resources are thoughtfully managed and accounted for?

Active appreciation for the value of human creativity, labor, and toil can be key to a healthy and happy enterprise. New methods of accounting will look at a variety of human and environmental debts and assets. These in-depth assessments will create a more holistic understanding of what a business contributes to and spends of its human and environmental resources. Many businesses of the future will seek new forms of ownership so as to distribute wealth more equitably. This has already begun.

... when businesspeople become consciously aware of themselves as creators of cultural and moral effects in society?

In my view, advertising has become one of the most pernicious forms of mind control that the world has ever known. Thoughtlessly it has encouraged addictions to food, alcohol, and tobacco, all in the name of financial greed. Young men and women have become objectified, their self-esteem and confidence dispirited. The human need for love, security, and acceptance has been exploited by advertising, again in the name of financial gain and greed.

Businesses of the future will engage their power to right this wrong, and will utilize mass media for the promotion of simple health and well-being on a global scale. This has already begun.

. . . when business becomes actively concerned for the health and well-being of its stakeholders and their families?

It has already been proven by innovative, values-driven companies such as Ben and Jerry's Homemade Inc., the Stride Rite Corporation, Starbucks Coffee Company, and others, that paying attention to the concerns and needs of employees with family responsibilities has a dramatic effect on employee morale, commitment, and productivity. Businesses of the future will gladly implement family-friendly policies and programs that create a more humane workplace. If it's good for people you can bet it will be good for business!

. . . when business takes to heart the principle of sustainability and works to create products and practices conforming to sustainability doctrines?

If a business cannot function without debasing nonrenewable natural resources, it will either find alternative modes of operation or cease to exist. New businesses will be founded and new products developed according to an evaluation of criteria for product merit, including environmental and social costs and benefits.

Extensive work regarding this topic is currently being done by The Natural Step, a nonprofit educational organization committed to furthering the goals of sustainable production.

So, you see, this too has already begun.

Finally, what will happen when all businesses are led by conscientious people who are imbued with common sense and are fully aware of their responsibility to allow and enhance the natural evolution of all life?

The road that we wish to follow to our desired destination of wellness will be traveled by businesses large and small. The success of the journey truly lives within the ability of each individual to learn of, understand, and live by natural principles. It is only through this understanding that we may hope for the continuation of living systems and communities upon our beautiful Earth.

This, I am happy to say, has already begun.

Creativity, adaptability, order and change, autonomy and control, structure and flexibility, planning and innovation — these are the cornerstones of living systems and business as well. Dare I ask what will happen when we humans become of one mind to integrate the wisdom of natural systems and natural care into our science, technology, medicine, education, politics, and commerce?

This book is my hope and prayer to inspire many to create natural businesses that will do exactly that.

LEAD ON WITH THE LIGHT

Adams, Bob. *Adams Streetwise Small Business Start Up.* Holbrook, MA: Adams Media Corporation, 1996.

Block, Peter. *Stewardship: Choosing Service over Self-Interest.* San Francisco: Berrett-Koehler, 1996.

————. *The Empowered Manager: Positive Political Skills at Work.* San Francisco: Berrett-Koehler, 1993.

Boldt, Laurence. *Zen and the Art of Making a Living.* New York: Penguin Books, 1993.

Bridges, Carol. *The Medicine Woman's Guide to Being in Business for Yourself.* Nashville, IN: Earth Nation Publishing, 1996.

Chopra, Deepak. *The Seven Spiritual Laws of Success.* San Rafael, CA: Amber-Allen Publishing, 1995.

Choquette, Sonia. *Your Heart's Desire.* New York: Three Rivers Press, 1997.

Cohen, Ben. *Ben & Jerry's Double Dip.* New York: Simon and Schuster, 1997.

Covello, Joseph. *The Complete Book of Business Plans.* Naperville, IL: Sourcebooks, 1994.

Edwards, Paul. *Teaming Up.* New York: Putnam Publishing Group, 1997.

Fields, Rick. *Chop Wood, Carry Water.* New York: Putnam Publishing Group, 1984.

Gladstar, Rosemary. *Herbal Healing for Women.* New York: Simon and Schuster, 1993.

Hawken, Paul. *Growing a Business.* New York: Simon and Schuster, 1987.

————. *The Ecology of Commerce.* New York: Simon and Schuster, 1987.

Kamoroff, Bernard. *Small Time Operator.* Willits, CA: Bell Springs, 1996.

Loughrans, Joni. *Joni Loughran's Natural Skin Care.* Berkeley, CA: Frog, Limited, 1996.

Lyons, Dianne. *Planning Your Career in Alternative Medicine.* Garden City Park, NY: Avery, 1993.

Monroe, Paula Ann. *Left-Brain Finance for Right-Brain People.* Naperville, IL: Sourcebooks, 1996.

Ray, Paul H. *The Integral Culture Survey.* Sausalito, CA: Institute of Noetic Sciences, 1996.

Roddick, Anita. *Body & Soul.* New York: Crown Publishing, 1994.

Root, Hal. *The Small Business Start-Up Guide.* Naperville, IL: Sourcebooks, 1998.

Sarner, Mark. *Social Marketing for Business.* New York: Manifest Communications, 1998.

Schumacher, E. F. *Small Is Beautiful.* New York: HarperCollins, 1989.

Toms, Justine. *True Work.* New York: Crown Publishing, 1998.

Wheatly, Margaret J. *A Simpler Way.* San Francisco: Berrett-Koehler, 1997.

————. *Leadership and the New Science.* San Francisco: Berrett-Koehler, 1992.

A Sample Purchase Order

SunFeather Natural Soap Company
1551 State Highway 72
Potsdam, New York 13676

Tel: (315) 265-3648
Fax: (315) 265-2902

Purchase Order

The following number must appear on all related
correspondence, shipping papers, and invoices:

P.O. NUMBER:

To:

Ship To:
SunFeather Natural Soap Company
1551 State Hwy. 72
Potsdam, NY 13676

P.O. DATE	CUSTOMER #	PLACED BY	SHIP VIA	TERMS

QTY	UNIT	DESCRIPTION	UNIT PRICE	TOTAL

SUBTOTAL	
VAT	
SHIPPING & HANDLING	
OTHER	
TOTAL	

1. Please send two copies of your invoice.
2. Enter this order in accordance with the
   prices, terms, delivery method, and speci-
   fications listed above.
3. Please notify us immediately if you are
   unable to ship as specified.
4. Send all correspondence to:
   Business Manager
   SunFeather Natural Soap Company
   1551 State Hwy. 72
   Potsdam, NY 13676

Contributors and Their Businesses

AmyLee
c/o Talon
3885 South Decatur, Suite 2010
Las Vegas, NV 89103

Artha Handmade Hempseed
  Oil Soaps
Allysyn Kiplinger
P.O. Box 20154
Oakland, CA 94620
(510) 420-0696
Hand, body, and shaving soap made with hempseed oil, including soap made in the shape of the Venus of Willendorf.

Aunt Bee's Skin Care
Karl Halpert
P.O. Box 2678
Ranchos De Taos, NM 87557
(505) 737-0522
Aunt Bee's lip balm, private-label lip balm, salves, solid perfumes.

Beaver Creek Productions
Bruce and Linda Gillette
R.R. #1 Box 138
Golden Valley, ND 58541
(701) 948-2229
Genuine handmade buffalo soap, custom leather tanning.

Falls Creek Soap Works
Gretchen Stangl-Charlton
1461 West Hurley-Waldrip Road
Shelton, WA 98584
(360) 427-1757
Handcrafted soaps.

Finger Lakes School of Massage
  & Aromatherapy Certification
  Program
Andrea Butje, Cindy Black
1251 Trumansburg Road
Ithaca, NY 14850
(607) 272-9024
Beginning and advanced education leading to national and New York state massage therapy licensing and aromatherapy certification; high-quality essential oils and aromatherapy products.

Gingham 'n Spice, Ltd.
Nancy M. Booth
4356 Biddeford Circle
Doylestown, PA 18901
(215) 348-3595
Wholesale and retail business selling dried herbs, potpourri, fragrance and essential oils, and related products internationally. Also offers classes in perfumery.

Montage Skin and Body Studio
Dianne de la Garrigue Jones
923 North Sepulveda Boulevard
Manhattan Beach, CA 90266
(310) 376-9711
Handcrafted soaps, herbal bath bombs, and various bodycare products. Also offers spa treatments.

Sage Mountain Herbal Retreat
    Center & Native Plant Preserve
Rosemary Gladstar
P.O. Box 420
East Barre, VT 05649
(802) 479-9825
*Herbal home study education, herbal
health retreats and tours, herbal apprentice
program, United Plant Savers conference,
Women's Herbal Conference, herbal tinc-
tures, salves, skin cream.*

SunFeather Natural Soap Company
Sandy Maine
1551 Highway 72
Potsdam, NY 13676
(315) 265-3648
*Handcrafted soaps and shampoo bars for
men, women, children, and pets; soapmaking club and newsletter; home-party marketing plan.*

TKB Trading
Kaila Westerman
360 24th Street
Oakland, CA 94612
(510) 451-9011
*Natural colorants, glycerin, soapmaking
supplies.*

WiseWays Herbals
Mariam Massaro
Singing Brook Farm
99 Harvey Road
Worthington, MA 01098
(413) 238-4268
*Bath crystals, herbal salves, balms, oils,
teas, extracts, vinegars, and flower essences.*

Business Resources

American Home Business Association
4505 South Wasatch Boulevard
Salt Lake City, UT 84124
(800) 664-2422
Web site: www.homebusiness.com
*Provides comprehensive benefits and ser-
vices, education, training, and support for
home-based business owners.*

Business for Social Responsibility
609 Mission Street, 2nd Floor
San Francisco, CA 94105-3506
(415) 537-0888
Fax: (415) 537-0889
Web site: www.bsr.org
*BSR is a national association of busi-
nesses providing assistance to companies
seeking to implement policies and practices
that contribute to the long-term, sustained,
and responsible success of their enterprise
and that fairly balance the competing
claims of key stakeholders, their investors,
employees, customers, business partners,
communities, and the environment.
Also operates the Business for Social
Responsibility Education Fund
(BSREF).*

Business Spirit Journal and Conference
c/o The Message Company
4 Camino Azul
Santa Fe, NM 87505
(505) 474-0998
*Publishes a newsletter that integrates topics
of spirituality and the workplace, and
organizes annual International Conference
on Spirituality in Business.*

Co-Op America
1612 K Street NW, #600
Washington, DC 20006
(800) 58-GREEN
Web site: www.coopamerica.org
A nonprofit organization dedicated to addressing social and environmental problems through the economic system. Helps members find businesses that create jobs, care about their communities, engage in fair trade, and protect the environment; provides technical assistance to help those companies succeed and grow.

Direct Selling Association
1666 K Street, NW, Suite 1010
Washington, DC 20006-2808
Web site: www.dsa.org
(202) 293-5760
A national trade association representing companies that manufacture and distribute goods and services sold directly to the end consumer. The DSA has published a Code of Ethics, which spells out guidelines for companies and salespeople to follow in selling products, recruiting new salespeople, and working with salespeople.

Enterprise Corporation of Pittsburgh
2000 Technology Drive, Suite 150
Pittsburgh, PA 15219
(412) 687-4300
Fax: (412) 687-4433
Web site: www.enterprise.org
A private, nonprofit corporation, affiliated with Carnegie Mellon University and the University of Pittsburgh, dedicated to serving the needs of entrepreneurs in the Pittsburgh community and throughout the world.

Entrepreneurial Education
  Foundation
7555 East Hampden Avenue, Suite 501
Denver, CO 80231
(800) 689-1740
Web site: www.fastrac.org
Offers Premier FastTrac® business development workshops throughout North America.

The Future 500
801 Crocker Road
Sacramento, CA 95864
(916) 486-5999
A progressive business organization seeking to further the goals of the sustainable business agenda.

The Handcrafted Soapmakers Guild
215 13th Street SW
Bandon, OR 97411
Web site: www.soapguild.org
A trade organization dedicated to promoting and implementing standards of excellence among soapmakers of every level and educating the public about handcrafted soap.

The Herb Growing & Marketing
  Network
P.O. Box 245
Silver Springs, PA 17575-0245
(717) 393-3295
Web site: www.herbworld.com
A trade association/information service for herb-related businesses. Publishes the Herbal Connection, *a bimonthly trade journal, and the* Herbal Green Pages, *an annual resource guide. Offers free classifieds, annual conferences, seminars, liability insurance, and more.*

Independent Cosmetic Manufacturers
and Distributors Inc.
1220 West Northwest Highway
Palatine, IL 60067-1803
(800) 334-2623
Web site: www.icmad.org
A trade organization. Organizes work-shops and offers benefits to members.

International Society for
Ecological Economics
P.O. Box 1589
Solomons, MD 20688
(410) 326-7414
Web site: www.kabir.umd.edu/isee/
iseehome.html
A nonprofit organization that encourages the integration of economics and ecology into a transdiscipline aimed at developing a sustainable world.

National Federation of Independent
Businesses
53 Century Boulevard, Suite 300
Nashville, TN 37214
(800) 634-2669
Web site: www.nfibonline.com
An advocacy organization composed of small and independent business owners.

The Natural Step
Box 29372
San Francisco, CA 94129-0372
(415) 561-3344
Web site: www.emis.com/tns
A nonprofit environmental education orga-nization that seeks to build consensus on how we can become ecologically and econom-ically sustainable as a society. Organizes workshops for industry and publishes a quarterly newsletter called Compass.

Northwind Media Consultants
Legwurks Planning Software
Box 5960
Potsdam, NY 13676
(315) 268-6612
Legwurks is a fully interactive, multimedia instructional guide to the entrepreneurial process that facilitates the development of comprehensive and credible business plans.

Small Business Administration (SBA)
200 North College Street, Suite A2015
Charlotte, NC 28202
(800) 827-5722
Web site: www.sba.gov
Has more than one hundred informational bulletins on business management and provides sound legal and financial advice for beginners in business.

Young Entrepreneur's Organization
1321 Duke Street, Suite 300
Alexandria, VA 22314
(703) 519-6700
Web site: www.yeo.org
A volunteer group of business profes-sionals, all under forty years of age, and founders, cofounders, or controlling share-holders of companies with annual sales of $1 million or more, who support, educate, and encourage young entrepreneurs in building companies and themselves.

Periodicals and Catalogs

The ArtFair Sourcebook®
2003 NE Eleventh Avenue
Portland, OR 97212-4027
Web site: www.artfairsource.com
(800) 358-0445
A listing, rating, and tracking system to the best art and craft festivals nationwide; lists suppliers of tools, equipment, and materials.

Entrepreneurial Edge
(800) 357-5693
Web site: www.edgeonline.com
Interviews with today's hottest entrepreneurs, real-world business solutions, straight talk on how to build a thriving business in the '90s and beyond.

Home Business News
(740) 988-2331
Web site: www.homebiznews.com
Reveals proven, little-known ideas, methods, and inside tips for operating a lucrative home-based business. Electronic subscriptions available.

Inc. Magazine
(800) 234-0999
Web site: www.inc.com
Provides hands-on advice, case studies, and big-picture overviews of the state of small business in North America.

Natural Foods Merchandiser
(303) 939-8440
Web site: www.newhope.com
Trade publication for the natural foods industry.

Internet–Only Business Resources

Entrepreneur
Web site: www.entrepreneurmag.com
On-line small-business magazine and Web site with various business-related tips and information.

Finance Hub
Web site: www.FinanceHub.com
Offers extensive information on business finance with many links to additional resources.

Net Marquee Family Business
   Netcenter
Web site: www.nmq.com
A news and information resource for owners and executives in family-controlled businesses.

Small Business and Entrepreneur's
   Forum
Web site: www.businessforum.com
An independent informational and professional resource center for the owners and managers of emerging business, with many good links to other business resources.

Smart Business Supersite
Web site: www.smartbiz.com
Provides extensive business-related information and many links to other good sites.

Your Company
Web site: www.yourco.com
Covers a wide range of small-business topics, from teen business owners to retirement planning and marketing savvy.

Other Storey Titles You Will Enjoy

The Candlemaker's Companion, by Betty Oppenheimer. 176 pages. Paperback. ISBN 0-88266-944-X.

The Essential Oils Book: Creating Personal Blends for Mind and Body, by Colleen K. Dodt. 160 pages. Paperback. ISBN 0-88266-913-3.

Growing & Using Herbs Successfully, by Betty E.M. Jacobs. 240 pages. Paperback. ISBN 0-88266-249-X.

Growing Your Herb Business, by Bertha Reppert, founder of The Rosemary House. 192 pages. Paperback. ISBN 0-88266-612-6.

The Herbal Body Book: A Natural Approach to Healthier Hair, Skin, and Nails, by Stephanie Tourles. 128 pages. Paperback. ISBN 0-88266-880-3.

The Herbal Home Spa: Naturally Refreshing Wraps, Rubs, Lotions, Masks, Oils, and Scrubs, by Greta Breedlove. 208 pages. Paperback. ISBN 1-58017-005-6.

Milk-Based Soaps: Making Natural, Skin-Nourishing Soap, by Casey Makela. 96 pages. Paperback. ISBN 0-88266-984-2.

The Natural Soap Book: Making Herbal and Vegetable-Based Soaps, by Susan Miller Cavitch. 192 pages. Paperback. ISBN 0-88266-888-9.

Perfumes, Splashes & Colognes: Discovering and Crafting Your Personal Fragrances, by Nancy M. Booth. 176 pages. Paperback. ISBN 0-88266-985-0.

The Soapmaker's Companion: A Comprehensive Guide with Recipes, Techniques & Know-How, by Susan Miller Cavitch. 256 pages. Paperback. ISBN 0-88266-965-6.

These and other Storey books are available at your bookstore, farm store, garden center, or directly from Storey Books, 210 MASS MoCA Way, North Adams, MA 01247. or by calling 1-800-441-5700. Or visit our Web site at www.storey.com.